IT PAYS TO STEAL

IT PAYS TO STEAL

· · · · · *Maury Wills*

as told to Steve Gardner

PRENTICE-HALL, INC., ENGLEWOOD CLIFFS, N. J.

Second printing........June, 1963

Prentice-Hall International, Inc.
(*London, Tokyo, Sydney, Paris*)

Prentice-Hall of Canada, Ltd.

Prentice-Hall de Mexico, S. A.

To
Pete Reiser

What Makes Maury Run?

By Bobby Bragan*

IT HAS BEEN my good fortune to enjoy many thrills in the game of baseball. However, of the joys that have come my way on or off the diamond, the permission to write a few words about Maury Wills brings me a real deep-down satisfaction.

Maury and I first became acquainted in Spokane, Washington in July of 1958. I had assumed managership of the Pacific Coast League team there and Maury was its shortstop. Anyone could see that this slightly built, agile, fleet-footed, strong-armed infielder was a major leaguer everywhere but at bat. He was 25 years old, and had been playing in the minors for several years with greater success in the field than at the plate. He impressed me as having desire, intelligence, courage and just about everything you'd expect a potential big leaguer to have except the ability to hit the ball consistently. He was a right handed hitter with little sting.

Wills was always one of the first players to report to the ball park. This habit proved very important in his case. As it happens on almost every professional baseball team, it's the pitchers

* Bobby Bragan was Wills' manager at Spokane and later became one of his coaches with the Los Angeles Dodgers. He has been signed to manage the Milwaukee Braves for the 1963 season.

who take their batting practice first. They usually hit for some twenty-five minutes, then the "extras" or utility men do their swinging. The final forty-five minutes is consumed by the regular line-up.

It was not unusual for Wills to show up with a bat in his hand a half an hour before the pitchers were scheduled to take batting practice. So, with the bat boys and ball boys doing the shagging, my coach, Tom Saffell and I would take turns throwing off the rubber to the ambitious Maury. It was on such an occasion as this that Wills took a couple of swings from the left side of the plate. He didn't look bad either.

"You have just put your foot on it," I ventured as he walked out of the batting cage to allow the pitchers to take over the practice.

"Put my foot on what?" replied Maury.

"On the key to the big leagues for you," I continued. "The way you can run, throw and field, all you need to do is to be able to get on first base a little more often."

"I'll be out earlier tomorrow and every day afterwards," responded a very eager, more confident athlete.

He worked diligently for the entire home stand, some two weeks. Then we hit the road for a similar period. Upon our return to Spokane the same routine continued. Maury was bunting and hitting altogether from the left side in practice and gaining confidence as the days went by.

Another road trip was coming up shortly and was scheduled to start in Sacramento. I sauntered over to the likeable shortstop and suggested that when we got away from the home fans again, I felt he would be ready to start switch-hitting. He was more than ready to begin the experiment. Knowing him, I got the feeling that he didn't think there was any experimenting to be done. He was confident he could do the job without difficulty.

He got two hits the very first night at Sacramento and a half dozen more in the series, all batting left-handed. From then on there was no stopping Maury Wills.

That he helped the Dodgers to the National League pennant in 1959 is of record. That he became one of the most colorful players in the game, all baseball recognizes. That he came along at a time when the emphasis in baseball is on *power* and defied one and all with his speed is one of the most remarkable accomplishments of modern baseball.

I suppose Maury has always possessed that intuition so rare in ball players. Jackie Robinson had it. It just seems that no matter how much effort is made by the pitcher to hold him close to the base he still gets his "jump" or "quick start" for the next base. It is much the same on a hit ball that is bobbled by an outfielder. It seems that Wills has an added sense that permits him to take the extra bases. It's doubtful if there is anything he doesn't know about running bases.

Maury introduced me to his father in Philadelphia after a Dodger-Phillies game in 1960. It was the first professional game that Mr. Wills had seen Maury play. Of course, Maury stole a couple of bases for the home folks to keep things normal. But I recall saying to Maury's dad that this speedster he had raised in Washington, D.C., was a boy of whom he could be justly proud. So am I.

They tell you that behind any man's success lies a woman. I'm sure that Maury's wife, Gertie, has given him the encouragement he needed along his rough road to success.

No doubt there are many who have made contributions along Maury's steps to fame. A high school coach, a brother, a friend, a neighbor, teammate, a teacher or someone other than his parents and immediate family. Whether it was by design or accident, this much I know about Maury Wills. He is as loyal as he is dedicated. And *too often* I have been notified by sportswriters that Wills has been showering some of the credit on me for his climb to the majors.

I'd like to make one point clear. It was in Maury Wills to become a star from the start. A guy can't have as many qualifications mentally and physically as he does and fail to make it big. He is the man who has made larceny pay. It is his legs, his eyes, his intuition, his reflexes, his savvy, his cunning, his dedication, his unique abilities that have established him as the greatest baserunner this game has known.

Again, it is one of the nicest things that has ever happened to me to be able to place these words in front of Maury's and I know that all who read *It Pays To Steal* will derive not only pleasure but insight into what makes Maury run!

Contents

IT PAYS TO STEAL

chapter • 1

Washington, D.C.

"Go, MAURY, GO," they hollered as I sprinted for second base, going in standing up ahead of the throw from the catcher. The playground was asphalt so I couldn't slide. The baseball was a tennis ball, the bat a broomstick. Paper bags with pockets in them were our gloves. I was only six years old, but I could run faster than many boys twice my age. I've been running ever since, but now I go into second base on my side with a twisting slide, hooking my foot, or I go in on my stomach, grabbing the bag with my hand as I slip by.

I was born in Washington, D.C., October 2, 1932. I was one of five brothers, and we had eight sisters. We didn't have expensive equipment—not even gloves like those my own boys have today. We organized our own games, developed our own talents, and, in spite of the primitive conditions, always managed to have a good time. Later, when I competed in the playground league, they furnished us with bats and balls.

My father was a Baptist minister who, in addition to his clerical duties, worked full time as a Government machinist at the Washington Navy Yard. Mother, also employed by the Government, was an elevator operator. I still marvel at the fantastic job they did in raising 13 kids on such limited salaries. They worked continuously, never had a vacation, and enjoyed few luxuries. As children we always had what we needed but didn't have everything we wanted. I've learned that you don't miss anything if you've never had it. I felt that everything was adequate. We ate well, had proper clothing, and received special presents at Christmas and Easter.

I try, like many other parents, to give my children some of the things I lacked. I also try to teach my children the importance of responsibility. They have been taught to save and use some of their allowance money for school supplies and other necessities. Married before I graduated from high school, I learned at an early age to think of someone besides myself. I feel in my heart that I am as good a person as anyone. If I can raise each of my children as well as my dad raised me, I will be more than satisfied. A lot of this responsibility falls on my wife Gertrude because I'm away from home so much each year.

We didn't have a Little League program, and, as a result, lacked the enthusiasm for baseball that most boys have today. From a personal outlook, I took little interest in the game until 1947, the year Jackie Robinson became the first Negro to break into the major leagues. After that I began following the Washington Senators and their games in the American League.

My hero, however, was not Robinson. I admired smaller players in the game such as Phil Rizzuto of the Yankees and Chick Pieretti, a vest-pocket pitcher with the Senators. I thought it was great that these men were competing on an equal basis with players who were 6 inches taller and 50 to 75 pounds heavier. Being small, I figured that if they could make the grade in the majors perhaps I could look forward to the same opportunity when I had completed my education.

When I was 14 I started playing hardball in a semipro league with grown men. I was a pitcher and had fairly good stuff. Prior to that time I had only played softball, a game that helped develop my coordination and other baseball skills.

We played on Sundays in the Washington area, in Maryland, and in Virginia. We received no compensation. That's when I first wore spiked baseball shoes.

When I was 15, I entered Cardozo High School (Washington) and played varsity football, basketball, and baseball. I played T-formation quarterback and was safety man on defense. We won the championship each year in football. You might say I was a scatback because I weighed only 150 pounds and stood only 5 feet 8 inches tall. My contention is that you don't have to be blessed with size to compete on an equal basis with larger boys—it's what you have inside that really counts. I always have had great desire, and I think that factor has made me every bit as big as anyone else on the field.

My high school baseball coach, Don Porter, started me off as a pitcher. He showed me how to throw a curve, how to improve my fast ball, and also taught me a lot about control. Fortunately, I had good aptitude for baseball, which combined with my semipro experience and his instruction left me farther advanced than most boys my age. I won my first high school start. It was a good omen because I went on to post a 25-2 record during the next three years, averaging from 15 to 18 strike-outs per game. When I wasn't pitching, I played third base. I hit well, too, averaging over .500 and getting my share of extra-base hits. I wasn't a singles hitter like I am today.

In each of my three years in high school I was fortunate enough to be selected to the all-high (all-city) teams in all three sports. When I graduated in June 1950 I was offered football scholarships by nine different colleges.

Aside from the normal amount of spike wounds, sprained ankles, black eyes, and facial bruises from ground balls, I've been remarkably free of serious accidents. My worst injury occurred while I was playing semipro ball in Washington. I was standing only five feet away from home plate when a bat flew out of a batter's hands and struck me above the right eye. I lost a pint of blood; several stitches were needed to close an inch-long gash. It took two days to stem the bleeding entirely. Fortunately the bat missed my eye or it might have ruined my vision.

My introduction to organized ball came that summer, 1950, when I was 17 years old. The *Washington Daily News* staged what was known as a "New-Talent Hunt." This was an annual affair held in Griffith Stadium while the Senators were on the road. From 300 to 400 boys with gloves and uniforms showed up for the tryout camp, and I was among them. Little did I realize then that I would not perform in a major-league ball park again until the Dodgers called me up from Spokane nine years later.

"All you men register, take a number, and go up in the stands. When we call your number, come down on the field. Don't call us. We'll let you know when your number comes up." These were the instructions which came over the public-address system.

Two hours passed, and I was still sitting in the grandstand waiting for my number to be called. Becoming impatient, I decided to take things into my own hands and tracked down the chief scout.

"Say mister, when can I have a chance to show you how I can pitch?" I asked timidly.

He gave me a startled look as if to say, "How did a little guy like you ever get in here in the first place?" To my surprise he motioned me to warm up on the sidelines. It was probably a desperation gesture to get me out of his hair. I don't know what he expected, but after a few pitches he was wearing a big smile. By then I had shown him a sharp-breaking curve, a good fast ball, and a deceptive change-up. He put me in the game.

They had split the group into two teams. Each pitcher was supposed to work two innings for his respective team before retiring to the grandstand to await further word—if any. I pitched my two innings and struck everybody out. Not one batter touched the ball. They announced on the P.A. that if any scouts wanted my name it was available. Every one of the then 16 major-league teams was represented at this clinic. Most of the batters I faced were high school and college boys from 17 to 21. One of the scouts asked to take another look at me. Back into the game I went and struck out the next three batters. This gave me nine straight strike-outs. Through it all my control was nearly perfect; only two pitches missed the plate.

As I walked toward the dugout, several scouts approached me and invited me to another tryout, a three-day session at Havre de Grace, Maryland. It was their final camp and was for boys considered to be definite professional prospects. I pitched five innings there, and my hot streak continued: I fanned all 15 batters! Not one of them even hit a loud foul ball. The scouts also organized sprint races for the players, and I outran everybody in camp. It was then that I learned that Brooklyn was interested in me. I also found out later that the New York Giants had been keeping tabs on me, but the consensus was that I was too small to be a major-league pitcher. When the Dodgers came to my home two weeks later I told them it would be a pleasure to join their organization.

At the time it was a difficult decision to make. I realized the importance of a college education then, as I do now. But there were other circumstances. For one, I had married my high school sweetheart, Gertrude Elliot, during our senior year on October 20, 1949, and I now had the responsibility of caring for two instead of just myself. We also were looking forward to becoming parents. Another factor was my burning ambition to become a major-league ball player. Before Jackie Robinson made good with Brooklyn and became one of the brighter stars in the National League, I hadn't really given it a thought. But his determination and eventual success gave me an incentive. I wanted to be a professional baseball player more than anything else in the world. Mine wasn't an easy journey to the majors, but, as I've learned since, it was well worth every sacrifice. If I had to start from scratch again, I'd make the same choice.

chapter · 2

Ministers Are Human, Too

WITH A BAPTIST minister for a father, my religious training started early. I attended church services on Sundays and every evening, seven nights a week, from the time I was five years old until I entered high school. After reaching high school, my evening schedule was curtailed and my Sunday attendance became irregular during baseball season when I started playing semipro.

My dad, Guy O. Wills, had a small parish of about 300 members. He has continued his preaching through the years and is just as dedicated today as he was when I was a boy. I send him a contribution for his church each month to show my appreciation for all he did for me during my boyhood days.

It was a rewarding experience to come from a large family. Dad did a lot to mold my character. He taught me to share with my brothers and sisters. We didn't have much opportunity to become selfish. We weren't spoiled either because we seldom had everything we wanted. We enjoyed our family life especially at Christmas and other major holidays when we all got together at one big dinner table. Mother prepared a big feast for these special occasions. They remain among my happier childhood memories.

My father's brother also was a preacher, and usually came over each Sunday before church. He conducted services right in our living room—preaching for an hour or more. This caused a minor conflict when my brother and I had to be at the ball park by 11 A.M. Rather than embarrass my parents, we slipped out the back door when we saw my uncle coming. Other times we jumped or dropped out of a second-story window because the door would be blocked with people. Some of our younger brothers and sisters didn't know why we were leaving but were smart enough not to say anything.

This early religious training has remained with me. I am conscious of the fact that there is a God and that we should always try to live according to His wishes. Religion is important to us especially in these trying times. Today when we have nothing else to turn to we are never alone if we really believe. This thought has carried over into my baseball playing and has provided me with strength when I am in need of a spiritual lift.

My being the son of a Baptist minister only proves and confirms my faith that religion is an individual belief. Just because my father was a preacher doesn't automatically make me a devout Christian. It is something I have had to acquire. I was blessed in 1959 when I joined the Dodgers and came in contact with the Rev. H. B. Charles, now my pastor.

Rev. Charles directs all activities at the Mt. Sinai Baptist Church on La Salle Avenue at West Adams Boulevard in Los Angeles. His parish numbers about 7,000, so he has quite a following. Through my association with him, I feel I have become a better person. I live with Rev. and Mrs. Charles during the playing season, an experience that has been worthwhile for me. All of us at one time or another are searching for something we lack or need. It may take only a spark to ignite a burning, driving force within us. It's difficult to define the personal illumination I have received from Rev. Charles, but it's something I lacked prior to our association.

When I mentioned that religion is an individual thing, I meant that one person might receive one particular message, another an entirely different inspiration, and yet a third still might gather a thought completely divorced from those of the other two. Through Rev. Charles' sermons I have absorbed countless divine benefits that have affected my career as a Dodger.

I remember a sermon he delivered which concerned God testing us. He used the automobile industry as an example— how a manufacturer will advertise that his car will do certain things; it will go so fast, get so many miles to the gallon, and perform in an intended way under specific conditions. But before these claims can be made the car first has to prove itself. So a test driver will take the car out, run it over the deserts in torrid weather, then up into the mountains in a cold climate. In watching a driver sending the car through these grueling tests you might think that he was punishing the car, trying to break it down, that he was fighting the car when actually he was for it. He only wanted to make the car prove itself that it could endure these rugged automotive requirements.

In the same way God makes us prove ourselves. At the beginning of the 1962 season I was missing balls that I normally would handle, making bad plays, giving a performance well beneath my ability. One would have thought that God was against me, that he was trying to punish me. But I know He was with me all the way. He's always with all of us. The question is: Are we with Him?

So with my faith in Him, I continued to do the best I could and kept striving for perfection. I think I proved myself to Him that I had faith regardless of how steep the road ahead looked. As a result, my playing changed completely. I experienced thrill after thrill during the 1962 season and I know without God's help and without inspiration from Rev.

Charles I wouldn't have had the memorable record-breaking base-stealing year in 1962 with the Dodgers.

My immediate family attends the Methodist Church in Spokane. All five of my children have excellent attendance records. The older ones haven't missed a day of Sunday school for the past seven years. My younger daughter hasn't missed in three years. I think this is wonderful because this is the Christian way of life which I believe in. Rev. Charles once told me:

"We are all Christians . . . so it doesn't really matter which church you attend . . . there's only one Father, the Heavenly Father."

When the Dodgers are on the road I seldom have a chance to attend services but I do visit other ministers. Rev. Charles has at least one clergyman friend in every National League city, many of them baseball fans. I call on them periodically but as our Sunday schedule calls for afternoon games, I have to be at the ball park by 11 A.M. Sometimes at home and on the road I am able to attend 8:30 morning services. Once in awhile I get permission to report late and can attend at 11 o'clock.

Rev. Charles is a rabid baseball fan and one of my biggest boosters. We've had several sports affairs at the Mt. Sinai Church at which time I have talked to the groups on baseball. They've presented me with several trophies and awards and have had special days in my honor at the church. Most of the church members are enthusiastic baseball fans. Preaching to this particular congregation is sometimes a real challenge for Rev. Charles because practically everybody at the 11 A.M. services (if the Dodgers are on the road) or at 3 o'clock when we're playing in Dodger Stadium has a transistor radio plugged into his ear. He has to be in top form to hold their attention. If the people feel that Rev. Charles is aware of their transistors, they'll post someone outside the door with a radio and he'll periodically peek inside to give the latest score by finger signs.

A fan himself, Rev. Charles at times will stop during a sermon to ask the score. On other occasions, if he is able to read the signs of the man posted outside the door, he'll interrupt himself to pass the score on to his congregation. I think it is wonderful for a minister to be so human, so regular, to take such an interest in a fine sport like baseball. I'm sure no one frowns on his stopping in the middle of his services for a baseball commercial.

I'm wondering if many people stay away from church because they feel they would rather be enjoying themselves doing something else. Church can show people how to enjoy themselves right there—how they can have complete enjoyment while worshipping. There is a fine fellowship associated with church, a relationship I never knew existed.

I know that more than ever God was with me during the 1962 season. I couldn't have accomplished what I did alone; I'm not that good. God helped me. He made it possible for me to break the record. I never hesitated, after each stolen base—104 of them—to thank Him immediately for helping me steal that base. When I make a good play or get a base hit —I thank Him each time for assisting me. I often say a prayer before the game. I ask God to give me the strength, courage, and determination to play hard and to give it my best. I can't ask for victory; that's out of His hands. If he grants my previous request there isn't much of a problem as far as winning is concerned.

If I know I gave my best I never feel bad after losing a ball game. Naturally no one likes to lose, and we've lost our share of tough ones. Perhaps had we shown more determination we might have won. If I feel that I could have done better and we lost, then I get pretty upset. You have to give the opposing players credit; God is with them, too, not the Dodgers exclusively. Perhaps the Giants, for instance, in the play-off games at the end of the 1962 season, were with Him a little more than we were. Maybe that's the reason they won. It's another way of looking at it. I've thought about it many times.

chapter • 3

Switch Hitting

IF SOMEONE HAD told me ten years ago that I would be a successful switch hitter, I think I would have questioned his mentality. I had enough trouble hitting from my natural right side to be thinking about batting from the other side of the plate. But in this game of baseball, just like the game of life, it pays to be open-minded—you've got to accept changes, especially if you can improve yourself.

Bobby Bragan was responsible for my success in becoming a switch hitter. I wasn't bunting as often as I should, I wasn't trying to hit the ball to opposite fields. I should have been trying to get on base any way I could. Once on base I could take advantage of my speed to score runs, to steal bases, to rattle the pitchers. Shortly after Bragan took over as manager at Spokane in July '58, he noticed me during batting practice and was not impressed. For some reason I moved to the left side of the batter's box, and, in fun, took a couple of cuts left-handed.

"Maury, have you ever tried hitting left-handed before?" he asked.

"No, Bobby, I've never given it much thought. I've had
all I could do to hit the ball right-handed," I answered.

"It's not so difficult as it seems. You might find it awkward
at first but once you master your coordination you'll be able to
get a free and easy swing at the ball. Why not try it?" he shot
back at me.

"Bobby, I'll try anything once."

For the next three days he worked with me, giving me
special batting practice before the rest of the team reported.
After the fourth day, he calmly announced that I was a switch
hitter.

While I don't necessarily recommend switch hitting to the
average ball player, this ambidextrous ability changed me
from a mediocre hitter to a good one. I had had my troubles
with the curve ball, especially with pitchers who side-armed
me on one pitch, then curved me with the next. I was stepping
into the bucket rather than into the ball. I wasn't getting
enough leverage in my swing.

My stepping away, I suppose, was a result of fear. You
can't be worried about getting hit with the ball. This comes
with experience, however, because now I have no fear at all.
I rely on my reflexes to get me out of the way of the ball. I
never think about getting hit. Once you think about the ball
hitting you, then you get on the defensive which is not the
proper frame of mind for a successful hitter.

In addition to the trouble I was having with the breaking
ball, Bragan wanted me closer to first base to take advantage
of my speed. The difference of being three feet closer to
first base can mean being safe or out on a close play. When
I was thrown out while batting righty, it was usually only by a
half a step or less, so the shorter distance proved to be ad-
vantageous.

I am now able to beat out a lot of infield hits which helps
my batting average. Some power hitters can bang the ball
off the fence and still be held to a single. I might dribble one
down the third-base line and beat it out. My effort won't be so

impressive, but at the end of the game both hits will look alike in the box score.

I've been able to overcome my weakness with curve balls, because when a right-handed pitcher throws me a breaking ball I now can see it coming to me from the moment he starts his delivery. With your head on a direct line when the pitcher starts throwing at you from the direction of third base, you get direct vision and a longer look at the ball. If I were batting right-handed against this same right-handed pitcher my vision would be slanted—I would be looking at the ball from an angle. That's another advantage of switch hitting—being able to see the ball coming to you from the split second it leaves the pitcher's hand.

A ball player with my speed should get at least 20 safe bunts a season. Before I became a switch hitter, I doubt if I was getting more than five or six each year. Although I don't get as many base hits on bunts as I'd like to, I've been able to shift the defense so that when the infielders move in tight, there are holes opened up for me to hit ground balls or high hoppers through or over the infield for base hits. For example, if the third baseman comes in too close all I have to do is punch the ball past him. If I can bounce the ball high on the first hop I can usually beat it out. If the shortstop goes over to back up the third baseman I try to hit it over second base. If the shortstop covers the middle I try to hit the ball through into left field. It's something I've had to work on continually, but it's paid off because I'm a better hitter today than I ever thought I'd be five years ago.

When the infielders shift, you have to adjust with them. Most ball players in the big leagues are smart—that's why they're up there. They give you nothing. You have to meet their challenge. I try to take advantage of these infield shifts in stealing bases. Junior Gilliam, one of the best switch hitters in the game, has worked the hit-and-run with me many times. He's able to anticipate where the defense will play him and has had the ability to "hit 'em where they ain't." Junior tries to hit behind me and usually is successful.

Had I been a strong hitter from the right side of the plate I probably wouldn't have tried to become a switch hitter. I had little choice. It was a last resort. If I had been getting enough hits and had a respectable batting average, I wouldn't have changed over. But Bragan knew that I could use my speed to advantage, and also felt I could learn with instruction and practice.

I've been asked by younger players if they should learn to switch hit. I tell them it's better to be a strong hitter from one side of the plate than to be a mediocre hitter from both sides. Younger players should concentrate on their stronger natural side. If their coach or manager decides they are not going to be exceptionally good hitters, then, and only then, should they try switch hitting. One reason younger players have never become successful switch hitters is that they are afraid of getting hit with the ball. To be a good hitter, this fear has to be eliminated.

There aren't too many switch hitters in the game today. You can count them on your fingers. There's Gilliam on our own club and Mickey Mantle and Tom Tresh of the Yankees to name a few. Some pitchers are able to switch hit, but not too many of them have perfected the art. Gilliam started out as a right-handed hitter, and switched over for the same reason I did. He has one of the greatest pair of eyes in baseball. Take a look at his record—you'll find he's probably been on base more times than any other player with a comparable batting average. Jim (Junior) seldom strikes out which brings up another important point for young players: no matter what you do at the plate try to hit the ball somewhere. Make the other team field it. When they have to handle it they can hurry their throws, the ball can take a bad bounce. Any number of things can happen to give you first base. But when you strike out you eliminate all these possibilities. In time I became a strong hitter from both sides because I had the pitches coming in to me. I could pick them up quicker, the pitchers couldn't side-arm me.

It's a great advantage to have a switch hitter coming up at a crucial time. The other manager can't juggle his pitchers to have a right-handed pitcher pitch to a right-handed batter and vice versa. When Jim Gilliam or I step up to the plate it doesn't make too much difference who they throw at us. If there's a lefty, I'll bat righty; if they switch all I have to do is walk over to the other side of the plate.

This often happens late in a ball game when the manager wants to make a pitching change. His pitcher may be getting tired. The manager might want to switch from a southpaw to a right-hander to face men like Tommy Davis and Frank Howard who will be following Gilliam in our batting order. Even though he knows his pitcher is weakening he'll leave him in because he knows I can switch. It's a break for me to get a chance to hit off a tired pitcher rather than a fresh one. It gives me a better chance.

Again my advice to young players: don't switch unless you absolutely have to. You take something away from one side when you switch. You've got to give up something to get something and you definitely sacrifice power when you go over to the unnatural side of the plate. It's a fact: something's got to give!

Oddly enough, while I'm naturally right-handed I feel that I'm a better left-handed hitter now. I have been averaging over .300 from the left side, but well under that from the right side. Approximately 75 to 85 per cent of the pitchers in the National League are right-handed, so in batting from the left side I have two great advantages: a shorter distance to first base, and I can see the ball longer and better.

Of the few home runs I've hit, most of them have been right-handed. I have more strength, can generate more power from my natural right side, but from my left side I hit the ball sharper and more frequently.

One night during the 1960 season I was clowning with

John Griffin, our veteran clubhouse chief, after I had helped win a tough ball game. By way of celebration I told Grif that if I ever hit two home runs in one game I'd buy him two boxes of cigars. This seemed like a safe bet at the time because my total homer output in the majors was a blazing zero. But a funny thing happened to me in the Polo Grounds on Memorial Day 1962—I hit a line-drive home run inside the park while batting left-handed off Bob Moorhead in the fifth inning, then in the ninth inning, batting right-handed, I hit a ball off Wilmer Mizell into the upper deck.[1] While I sat sipping a cold drink following the double-header in the centerfield clubhouse, Grif handed me a printed message which read:

TWO BOXES OF GOLDEN WEDDING CIGARS—
50 IN A BOX AS PER AGREED IN 1960

JOHN GRIFFIN

I'd forgotten the promise, but he had me trapped; I gave him his cigars. I'd like to pay this bet off about 30 times a year, but I'd have to add about 50 pounds so I hardly think it's worth considering. Every time I hit a home run Walt Alston is the first to caution me not to start swinging for the long ball. Players have a penchant to try for distance once they have boomed a few over the fence. I'm not interested in hitting home runs. If all my hits were homers, I wouldn't get to run. Just think how lonely I'd feel if the fans stopped shouting "Go! Go! Go!"

[1] Wills became the fourth player in the National League and sixth in the majors to hit one home run right-handed and another left-handed in the same game.

chapter 4

Long, Long Trail
to the Majors

HAVING BEEN NOTIFIED by the Dodgers that I had been assigned to the Class D Hornell club, I left Washington by train in March with several other rookies and arrived in spring training at Dodgertown, Vero Beach, Fla., along with some 400 other players. The Dodgers had the largest farm system in organized baseball with 20 ball clubs ranging from Class D to the major-league entry represented.

The Hornell (N.Y.) team was one of several lower-classification clubs in camp. When I reported for my first workout, there must have been 250 players on the same field. Here I was, my first time away from home, not much bigger than a grammar-school boy, and scared to death.

"We'll start off with all you men lining up in your respective positions," barked one of the instructors with a battery-operated hand megaphone. "All of the catchers form a line in back of the plate, the first basemen go to first, the second basemen to second, and so on. All pitchers line up by the third base dugout."

As I trotted over with the pitchers it seemed as though there were 200 of us. Most of the men were large enough to make me look like a midget. In glancing over the infield I noticed there was only one second baseman so I went over to the instructor with a request to join the infielders.

"Say coach, I can play second," I stammered.

"My name isn't coach, it's Doc Axelson. I'm your manager. Go ahead and try it, kid," he replied.

Four days later, after hours of infield practice, I was still anchored at second base. When I reported on the field that day I tracked Doc down to see if I could still try out as a pitcher.

"Kid, the way you play that infield, you'd better forget about being a pitcher. Stay on second base, you're doing fine," he answered with a grin.

So just like that my pitching career came to a sudden end, and I started a new one as an infielder. It's debatable whether I would have been a successful pitcher. I know one reason I was relegated to the infield was because of my size. I didn't impress anyone. Most scouts, managers, and coaches look for big pitchers who can overpower the batters. Yet men like Elroy Face, Bobby Shantz, and Harvey Haddix are all little guys with impressive major league pitching records.

I don't know if I could have won consistently in the big leagues. I've been an infielder ever since I started in pro ball and have no regrets. I think I might have made it in the minors with my good control to go along with a curve and a fast ball. I know I'm a lot happier playing shortstop than I would be pitching. I like to play every day. If you're a pitcher, you get rotated every fourth day unless you're a reliefer—then there's no telling when you'll see action. If you're in the bull pen and the starter goes all the way, then they don't need you and you won't get into the line-up at all. Pitching has always been in my blood, though. I got a lot of personal satisfaction out of winning a game; there was a certain amount of glory associated with it, like hitting a home run.

At Hornell, a town with a population of 12,000, I played second base the entire 1951 season. Our club was in the

Pony League. Everyone treated me well, and I had a good season, hitting around .280 and stealing 54 bases. I was still short of the stolen-base mark of 63 which Don Zimmer had set the previous year. This proves another point I've been trying to make—that you don't have to be extremely fast to steal bases. Zimmer did not have blinding speed. Average speed is often all that is required.

I didn't need an armored car to take my salary to the bank on pay day. I was paid $135 a month after having received a $500 bonus for signing. The next year I received a raise and began taking home $200 a month. I was promoted to the Class C Santa Barbara club in the California League. I was still young enough to think that Santa Barbara was the end of the world so my request to spend another year at Hornell was granted.

Things went well for me. I hit .300, led the league in stolen bases with 54, and in hits and runs scored. I also made the all-star team. By now, the Dodgers had tabbed me as a definite major-league prospect and sent me to the Class A Pueblo (Colorado) club of the Western League.

The following year I moved up again, this time to the Fort Worth team in the Class AA Texas League. I was the first Negro to play at Fort Worth, and I had to learn to experience pressure off as well as on the field. People weren't exactly hostile, but I had a lot of adjusting to do. I had trouble finding places to eat. Proper housing and other obstacles caused me considerable difficulty. The fans were great, they treated me fine. But in traveling around the league I often had to seek my own accommodations. My teammates had reservations waiting for them, but mine weren't taken care of the way I felt they should have been.

I've found in baseball, as in anything else, that a person can't perform his best without a relaxed mind and body. You must have peace of mind because when you combine this condition along with an honest effort there's no limit to what you can accomplish.

That's why many times in baseball I'll set a goal—not just for personal satisfaction or glory—to help me to succeed, a constant reminder not to let down, to keep me driving for perfection. When I succeed as an individual the ball club benefits as well. If all nine players have big seasons the entire team is going to wind up on top. Outside of double plays, the hit-and-run, pick-off plays, and squeeze plays, baseball is a game of individual performances. There isn't the precision blocking required in football nor the intricate fast-break passing patterns associated with basketball; in baseball a player is pretty much on his own. It's up to him as an individual to come up with a peak performance. That's one reason I set goals and try to top them.

But, in 1955 at Fort Worth, I was down mentally. I was tensed up and lacked the confidence which comes from peace with one's inner self. I was having a bad year. By midseason I was only hitting around .220, so from the middle of June I spent the rest of the year on the bench. As a result of this slump, the Dodgers cut my salary and demoted me back to the Pueblo club the following year. It was a bitter pill to swallow and nearly caused me to lose faith in myself and baseball. It was a big blow to my career. As a family man I couldn't afford the cut in salary and the demotion didn't exactly give my spirits a lift. But with the choice of quitting baseball or going home I realized my obligations. So rather than give up the game I loved, I went back to Pueblo with renewed determination to have a good season. I knew if I could bounce back I would be drafted by another ball club. Each ball player is entitled to three options, and my three had expired. I was certain this could be the break I was seeking provided I could play well enough to earn it. I couldn't have planned it better. I hit .302, led the circuit in stolen bases with 34, hit 10 home runs, and made the all-star team. And, as I predicted, I was drafted. Seattle of the Pacific Coast League became my next stop.

Seattle had a working agreement with the Cincinnati Redlegs, so I assumed I was now a member of their farm system. Later I found out the Dodgers still owned me. As a rookie in Triple A ball at Seattle in '57 I had a pretty good season hitting .267, fielding well, and stealing 21 bases. I heard that several clubs were interested in me, but the Dodgers exercised their claim, and I was sent to Spokane.

I had come to the crossroads, and, although I didn't realize it at the moment, this switch to Spokane proved to be one of the big turning points in my life. One reason was an association with an inspiring field leader named Bobby Bragan. Bobby took over as the manager at Spokane in the middle of the '58 season. He took a big interest in me and just being around him made my baseball life worth living. At the time I was floundering. I had just about given up on myself, and the dedication it takes to excel and move up the ladder was disappearing. Apparently I would never be more than a good minor-leaguer. Strange as it seems, I lacked little as far as ability was concerned. I could throw as well then as I can now, possibly even better. I wasn't hitting too well but I could run as fast and my fielding was as good as it is today. I was down mentally. But this was before I met Bobby Bragan.

Bobby helped me regain the confidence I had lost in myself. I had just been going through the motions, doing enough to get by, grinding out an adequate living for my family. He gave me the spark, the extra charge I needed to get out of my rut. With my faith and desire restored I wound up the season stealing 25 bases and finishing strongly enough to earn an invitation to join the Detroit Tigers in spring training the following March in Lakeland, Fla.

The possibility of going to Detroit gave my spirits a big boost and justified everything Bobby Bragan had told me about improving my attitude. I started to enjoy playing again and was looking forward to finally reaching the big time. My immediate goal was to better myself, which was a great incentive. So when I reported to the Tigers I gave them everything I had and plenty to spare. In effect, I was a human tiger with a dedicated desire to succeed.

So with all this renewed vigor I must have looked like the original eager beaver. I was at the ball park two hours ahead of everyone and stayed two hours after practice had concluded. What else did I have to do? This was my profession and I was determined to make good. This was too great an opportunity to miss. I worked on my fielding and perfected countless other techniques. When I was through with the routines the Tiger coaches prescribed, I asked them if there was anything else they wanted me to do. I wasn't satisfied doing just enough to get by. Had report cards been issued, I would have received an A for effort.

During the exhibition season I hit just under .500 with 11 hits in 23 times at bat, I stole eight straight bases, and fielded almost flawlessly. I hustled every second and improved my hitting from the left side of the plate. (Bragan had encouraged me to become a switch hitter the previous summer.) But Detroit decided to return me to the Dodgers, and two days before the start of the 1959 season sent me back to Spokane.

The Tigers had a name shortstop in Rocky Bridges, one reason I was rejected. In baseball a name goes a long way. The ball player with a name has proven himself; his manager knows what he can do. He may not be a big star, but he's shown he can get the job done. Without previous major-league experience, I was an unknown quantity. The Tigers didn't want to gamble on me in spite of my brilliant play during spring training. Furthermore, no one had ever heard of me. I didn't have a big name. I saw Rick Ferrell, the Detroit general manager, several months later and he admitted the Tigers made a mistake in not keeping me. I didn't blame Detroit, however, because how could they know I would ever become a major-leaguer? I know I'm a much better ball player now than I was back in spring training in '59; in fact, several scouts have told me that I'm the most improved player they have seen in years, which, of course, is nice to hear. While I couldn't understand why the Tigers didn't keep me, I didn't question their judgment either. By this time I was well-conditioned for letdowns and heartbreaks, and if I wasn't destined for the majors there wasn't any place I'd rather wind up than with Bragan at Spokane.

chapter • 5

Next Stop—
Los Angeles Dodgers

"It's a long, long time from May to December . . ." and it's even longer from March 1951 to June 1959. After eight years in baseball I had been through the wringer of trial and error, triumph and failure, frustration and elation. There were days when I thought I was on top of the world, others when I was ready to keep right on running until I reached home in Washington, D. C.

Most rookies break into the majors when they are in their early 20's. However, when I first put on a Dodger uniform I was nearly 28. My own explanation for coming to the Dodgers late in my career is because of the manner in which I was signed and the man who signed me.

Just like ball players, scouts also move from one club to another, and Rex Bowen was no exception. Shortly after he had signed me to a Dodger contract, he left our organization and joined the Pittsburgh chain when Branch Rickey became a major stockholder with the Pirates.

When a scout signs a player, he watches him closely. He follows his progress in the different classifications—mothers him along and tries to push him up through the ranks as rapidly as possible. Should a scout discover a ball player who eventually makes good in the majors, his reputation as a keen judge of diamond talent increases considerably.

When Rex went to Pittsburgh I had no one to take a personal interest in me. I was like an orphan. There was no one in the Dodger organization who could give me the front-office help I needed. A scout would have to turn to his reference files to find out anything about me.

Another reason my name was probably relegated to the minor-league card file was my insignificant size. I just wasn't impressive. Today's professional athletes in football and basketball seem to be three or four inches taller than the average player of the 1940's, and baseball has followed the same trend.

For every little guy in baseball today, I can name about a dozen or more big men who seem to dominate the game—players like Jim Gentile of the Orioles, Barry Latman and Rocky Colavito of the Indians, Norm Siebern of the Athletics, Ralph Terry of the Yankees, Ernie Broglio and George Altman of the Cards, Dick Stuart of the Red Sox, Vernon Law and Don Cardwell of the Pirates, Orlando Cepeda and Willie McCovey of the Giants, Joey Jay and Jim Brosnan of the Redlegs, and Frank Howard and Don Drysdale of the Dodgers. They are big, rugged men who tower over six feet and weigh 200 pounds or more. Every major-league roster today is dominated by players who average six feet tall or better.

When I found myself in the middle of this new generation of supermen, about the only thing I could do to catch a scout's eye was to run. If he would continue to take an interest in me I could show him a few other things such as fielding and throwing. But at 5 feet 10 inches and 150 pounds I had a tough time making a strong first impression.

That's why it was a big break for me to play for Bobby Bragan at Spokane. When I returned from my unsuccessful bid to hook on with the Detroit Tigers, Bragan resumed his sponsorship of me and kept my spirits soaring. He had given me so much confidence the previous year that my failure to make the Tiger club didn't faze me a bit. In one respect it was a blessing in disguise to be back at Spokane where Bobby continued to groom me for the majors. I don't know who said that opportunity knocks but once—it doesn't matter because I was tapped twice.

With our season at Spokane one-third gone, I found myself, after 48 games, hitting a nifty .313, I had stolen 24 bases, and was enjoying my finest year in baseball. You can imagine my inner delight when it was rumored that I was being called up by the Dodgers. I first learned that something was in the air when we stopped briefly at the Los Angeles International Airport on our way to Phoenix. One of the players had bought a paper at the newsstand and was reading it when he returned to the plane. He found an article that said I was to replace Bobby Lillis as shortstop for the Dodgers. Several players came by my seat to show me the story. It was a complete surprise, but after being let down so many times in the past including my recent rejection from Detroit, I wasn't going to get carried away with my own enthusiasm.

"Bobby, is this article true? Do you think the Dodgers are really going to send for me?" I asked Bragan. He answered:

"Maury, it looks like you've finally made it. I put in a strong recommendation for you to Buzzie Bavasi the other day on the phone. I haven't heard anything to date, so let's just play it by ear. He did say he needed another shortstop, and I told him you were his man, that you were ready."

But the days dragged on, and I still hadn't received any word. We had played three games in Phoenix (San Francisco Giants farm club in the Pacific Coast League—now Hawaii), and it looked like the news of my moving to the big leagues was a bit premature. Finally on June 1st, I received a wire from Mr. Bavasi in Los Angeles instructing me to report to Dodger manager Walter Alston in Milwaukee. I said goodbye to Bobby Bragan, thanked him for all he had done for me and "floated" to the airport.

So my own personal D-Day—Dodger Day—had finally arrived. As our plane left Sky Harbor in Phoenix headed east to Milwaukee, I bowed by head in silent prayer. The stewardess brought me a cup of coffee. I was so nervous I could hardly keep my hand from shaking while I drank it. It was almost like a dream to know that after all the detours I finally was headed in the right direction.

When the plane landed in Milwaukee, the players already had gone to the ball park. I caught a cab and made quite a comical entrance at County Stadium. I didn't have my regular duffle bag that we use to carry our equipment, so my shoes, my glove, and the rest of my gear were thrown together in a flimsy cardboard box. As I walked into the clubhouse, several of the Dodger players stopped to ask if I had brought my lunch. I didn't feel like a stranger, fortunately, because I knew most of the players from our spring-training days in Vero Beach.

I located my locker and above the stall was amused to find they had printed my formal name—"Maurice." I'm not superstitious, but I have always used this name on my locker while I've been with the Dodgers. It pleases me because it's a happy and constant reminder of my first day in the major leagues, a memory I'll treasure as long as I live.

After dressing nervously I walked through the tunnel underneath the stands which led to our dugout, my spikes clicking on the cement and my heart pounding. Alston greeted me warmly, and we went out on the field for a pregame television interview. When questioned I told him that I felt fine, had come to play, and was ready to help the team in any way possible. I also said I wasn't nervous over the promotion and that I thought I could play as well in the majors as I had in the minors at Spokane.

"You'd better sit out the first game, Wills. You'll have a chance to observe the way we play from the bench, then you can start the second game," advised Alston.

I'd have to be a little blasé not to have experienced a genuine thrill when the public-address announcer said, "Maury Wills, Shortstop," when he came to my name in the line-up for the second game. I'd always thought I'd be nervous in my first game and rightfully so—I was really keyed up. I guess everyone expected me to be a little tense. I didn't disappoint them: I made two errors. I knew everyone back in Washington D.C. and in Spokane would be watching because we were playing the TV Game of the Week. Even though I didn't get any hits I felt that I performed well, especially on a play which ended the game when I went far to my left in back of second base to throw out Eddie Mathews. As I recall we won the game, 3-2.

The news that I had been picked up by the parent club didn't exactly capture the imagination of the Los Angeles sportswriters covering the Dodgers. Here are some excerpts from an article which has given me a laugh every time I read it:

DODGER BIG DEAL
SEEMS RIDICULOUS

Cincinnati—June 2—Maury Wills for Bobby Lillis! That's the big deal the Dodger brass pulled off in an effort to keep the club in the first division. Who are they kidding? Maury Wills, 25 years old, has been bumping around in the minors since 1951. He's a good AAA ball player. Latest Coast League figures available show he was batting .313 for Spokane and had stolen 24 bases. Last year with the PCL team he hit only .235 and couldn't stick with Detroit this spring after being sold to the Tigers on a conditional basis. They returned him. The player he couldn't beat out was Rocky Bridges, himself cast off by the Dodgers after performing infrequently in a utility capacity. Wills may not even break into the line-up for a spell.

One of the most disturbing elements of my debut with the Dodgers was my inability to get a hit the first 12 times at bat. Finally on my 13th time I collected a single, but after two more times at bat they benched me. Had I been a regular or a name player and had picked up only one hit in 15 attempts, no one would have given it too much thought. But being a rookie and with no major-league experience, it was taken for granted that I couldn't hit major-league pitching. I knew differently and could only hope that the Dodgers would not give up on me these first few days. The pitching I saw wasn't too much sharper than that I had faced in the minors. They didn't seem to throw any harder and the curves didn't break any better. I was certain that in time I would start hitting the ball. Not too many ball players pop into the majors and set the league on fire, especially with a club the caliber of the Dodgers. Willie McCovey, who was called up that same summer from Phoenix by the Giants, was a notable exception.

Another interesting article written by one of the Southern California baseball columnists on July 19, 1959, described my plight fairly accurately:

> Maury Wills must wonder if he's hitting an iron ball and if opposing infielders are carrying magnets in their gloves. The rookie Dodger shortstop with the fancy handle on the glove has yet to solve Wee Willie Keeler's formula of "hit 'em where they ain't." More often Wills hits them where they "is," and the result shows in his .206 batting average. Ten times since he joined the Dodgers on June 6 Wills has been robbed of base hits with line-drive outs. Had six of these liners dropped for hits and with a normal amount of luck he would have been batting .302. Such bad luck has discouraged other rookies but Wills has managed to keep his chin high in the air.
>
> "I feel that I have been accepted and that I'm part of the club now," Wills said before Saturday's game. "The pressure was great during the first couple of weeks. Everyone had an eye on me. I felt I had to produce or I'd be back in Spokane." The first dozen games Wills was as shaky as a bowl of jelly that hadn't jelled.

Over a month had gone by since I put on a Dodger uniform, and I was still having my troubles at the plate. I was confident of my ability to hit, but apparently I was pretty much alone in my thinking. Another Los Angeles baseball writer came up with this observation:

SHORTSTOP SITUATION CRITICAL

Chicago—Aug. 13—If the Dodgers are to battle their way past the Giants and hold off the Braves in this pulverizing pennant scramble, something must be done about the shortstop situation. Maury Wills is hitting .211 and in 45 games has batted in only one run. His advertised golden glove has not compensated for his total lack of punch. I don't see how manager Walt Alston can go along without doing something about it. Admittedly this is easier written then done. Apparently there is nothing in the farm system that Alston and Buzzie Bavasi figure would be the answer. That leaves just one solution, Don Zimmer. Zip, fuming and muttering at being sentenced to the bench, has been a bust at the plate this year, too. However, there may be extenuating circumstances. He has not been in there for any continuous stretch. Each time he has been given the call, Zimmer has been pressing because of the shadows of first Bob Lillis and then Wills. In 123 at bats, Wills has hit in just one run. The Dodgers need punch more than any other single thing. You don't spell punch W-I-L-L-S. . . . The team is crying for power, some sort of change has to be made.

But the Dodgers kept me and after alternating with Don Zimmer during June and July, I finally nailed down the starting shortstop assignment by the middle of August. Then came one of the high spots of the entire season (both for the Dodgers and for me personally): a three-game series in San Francisco with the hated Giants. They were having Pacific Festival Week and as part of the celebration an airline company had offered a free trip for two to Japan for the most valuable player in the series. I collected seven hits in thirteen trips, hit .538, scored four runs, and was voted the winner by the sportswriters. I wasn't able to visit Japan, but nevertheless it was a great honor to be selected.

It was also a big thrill for me to be selected over such name players as Willie Mays, Duke Snider, Gil Hodges, Wally Moon, and Don Drysdale. It was equally exciting to have the Dodgers sweep the series because it proved to be the turning point of the flag race. The Giants never recovered, and from then on we were rolling toward the championship.

Our team play continued to be brilliant, and at the end of the regular National League season we found ourselves deadlocked with the Milwaukee Braves with identical 86-68 records. As the regular shortstop I began to realize how fortunate I was to be a member of a winning team my first season in the big leagues. I had a few butterflies fluttering in my stomach when the play-off series started in Milwaukee. It hadn't been too many weeks since I had left the minors. I began to feel a little pressure but knew I wasn't alone. Even some of the old pros were pressing. Good athletes perform better when they experience some nervousness. That's why many top clubs have trouble with second-division teams. The players can't get themselves emotionally high enough to play winning baseball.

Most players are at their best in front of a large crowd. It's almost like play-acting. If there's a large, appreciative audience, players turn in noteworthy performances. Often a small crowd doesn't generate enough enthusiasm to get them up. That's why you can't depend on crowds or any other outside factor to get you into the positive mental condition for a ball game. If you start letting external interests bother you, you're apt to turn into a streak hitter. A real champion is able to perform consistently. To do that, you've got to be fired up with a will to win. That's one of the most exacting assignments we face as major-leaguers. If we only played when we felt like it we'd spend quite a bit of time on the bench. You have to put yourself in a proper frame of mind.

I still regard my '59 season as a fortunate turn of events.

Had I joined the Detroit team I'd have been among the also-rans. Not only did I wind up with the National League champions, but by the middle of October was a member of the world champions. Many players, great stars like Ernie Banks, for example, who have been in the game for years, never have had the opportunity to play on a winning ball club. So when I found myself in the middle of the World Series I almost felt like pinching my leg to realize what actually had happened to me in comparatively four short months.

It didn't dawn on me at the time that this was such a great honor. I guess I was too busy playing to appreciate the importance of it all. I almost took playing in the World Series for granted. I enjoyed getting a big, fat check, and I felt honored to play in the Series, but the significance didn't really sink in until the following year when the Pirates edged the Yankees. As I was sitting home watching the games on television, it occurred to me that here was a select group of ball players, each of them a champion in his own right and rightfully honored to be represented in a World Series that for a chosen few comes only once in a lifetime.

Some young players possibly have gone through the same emotional experience that I did. They might have taken the league pennant and the World Series in stride, enjoying the distinction only because they were told it was a privilege to play in one. That's the only reason they thought it was wonderful, because they were told that it was. It's like believing in God. You don't believe because your pastor tells you to, it's something you must experience for yourself. Then you know you believe in Him because you've communicated with Him.

I can't wait to get into another World Series. We've had two near misses in recent years. It was a big disappointment to get within three outs of the '62 Series and we weren't too far away in 1961. We have a young ball club and from all indications the Dodgers are going to be the team to beat for the pennant for a good many years. So much goes with being in the Series. Not just money—that's important, too—but indescribable prestige and glory. You can't measure these in terms of material things, but mainly from a standpoint of personal satisfaction. And believe me when this fame doesn't come to you, you miss it. It's just like a finger. You'd miss it if it wasn't there, but as long as you have it you just take it for granted.

Sportswriters, announcers, and fans were generous in their praise of me in the Series. They compared me favorably with Luis Aparicio who was regarded as the No. 1 shortstop in baseball at that time. Several commentators reported that I outplayed Aparicio, which was flattering, but I still believe he is tops. I rate him today as one of the greatest, and think he deserves all the credit he received. However, I think I've improved to a point where I can set a goal to become the best shortstop in the major leagues.

My selection to the all-major-league team in a poll conducted by the Associated Press and United Press International was, of course, a great honor. Undoubtedly several of the men making the selections were influenced by my record-breaking total of 104 stolen bases. But I'm grateful for their recognition as well as that of the Most Valuable Player Award, and hope I can continue to be among the best, if not the best.

In looking back to my first season in the majors I remember some of the things that were said about me when I was down in the minors. Many baseball buffs said I'd never make it as a major-leaguer. Others said that if I did reach the majors I'd wind up as a utility player and that my stay would be a short one. I guess every player has heard these same abusive jabs at one time or another during his professional career. I can say truthfully I didn't relish these remarks, but I didn't let them discourage me either. If anything, they spurred me on. They gave me increased motivation to strive for success. It's not that I have an ax to grind, but it's been fun proving that a player such as I with a certain amount of God-given abilities can acquire even greater skills in furthering his cause for excellence.

A player doesn't have to throw a baseball a specific distance or hit the ball over 400 feet, but with proper coaching many other outstanding talents can be developed. Such was my individual case because if Bobby Bragan and Pete Reiser hadn't helped me obtain these other skills, I wouldn't be in the majors. As often happens in the game of life, timing is important. I was fortunate to be associated with these inspiring leaders in two successive seasons. I know there are many ball players with as much ability as I have, but they've never been able to improve their play because they haven't had this special instruction.

That's the reason I hope when my playing days are over that I can stay in baseball and teach young players the many benefits that I have acquired, even if I have to do it for nothing. I would feel I was cheating someone if I kept all of this knowledge bottled up inside of me and just turned my back on baseball—a game that has been so good to me and my family. I'm at the point now where I want to start giving back to baseball. If I can stick around long enough to do a good job with some of the promising young ball players on the way up, I will consider myself rewarded. One of my more enjoyable assignments was working with the Dodger rookies in the winter-league training program in Phoenix. I spent a few days there in November on a volunteer basis after the '62 season helping them with their base-running techniques. I could tell from their attitude that I was able to reach them, and this was all the thanks I needed.

chapter 6

Pete Reiser—
My Guiding Light

WHAT'S THE MARK of a true champion? Outside of an abundance of natural ability, I'd say complete confidence in reaching the top and then staying on top is the most important asset a champion can possess. Ted Williams and Jackie Robinson had it; they reeked with class. Willie Mays and Don Drysdale are examples of confident champions in the majors today. Another thing they have in common is that they are all great competitors. In time I'm hoping to add my name to their select circle. Confidence isn't something that comes to you in your sleep. It's something you develop with hard work, concentration, practice, and experience under game conditions. I've tried to develop a competitive spirit, because in baseball as in life it often spells the difference between victory and defeat.

There was a time, however, back in 1960, when I seriously doubted if I'd ever make the grade as a major-leaguer. While I had come up to the Dodgers with a good-field, no-hit reputation, my final weeks of the '59 season—including a fairly successful World Series—indicated I finally had arrived as a hitter. At least that's what I thought. But 1960 was a brand new season, and, while I had finished the '59 campaign on

50

top of the wave, I was now having more trouble than I bar-
gained for each time I stepped to the plate.

Regardless of a strong throwing arm, my ability to cover a
lot of ground, and to steal bases, few infielders who couldn't
hit over .220 ever have remained in the big leagues for any
length of time. That was the situation in which I found
myself when the season was only half completed. And it
seemed the harder I tried, the more I pressed, the more difficult it was to get a hit. As they say in the sport pages, I couldn't
buy a base hit. More than one Dodger fan had given up on
me, and my promising four months of 1959 were about to be
washed down the drain.

For those of you who follow baseball, I'm sure you can
sympathize with me when I tell you how humiliated I was to be
lifted constantly for pinch hitters. There's probably only one
thing worse: being knocked out of the box as a pitcher. I've
gone through that agony, too, because I broke into organized
baseball as a pitcher. One night they'd yank me in the seventh
inning; another time it would be the sixth. It was nearly more
than I could bear. Equally embarrassing was the location of
the Dodgers' official club box—located in the front row
directly on the home plate side of our dugout. So I'd pick up
my glove and my warm-up jacket and trudge past the front-
office brass night after night on my way to the showers in the
Coliseum tunnel. If I could have crawled I'd have done so.
These were without question among the most depressing
moments of my baseball career. Had it been possible to dig a
trench to the locker room I would have been willing to do so.

It is said that when you get as low as you can get there's
only one way to go—up. That isn't quite true. I've tried it,
and I know differently. Instead of being removed in the sixth
or seventh inning, I had hit a new low because now they were
taking me out for a pinch hitter in the third inning. I was
ready to call it quits. I simply couldn't take it any longer. I
wasn't helping the club, I was pressing, and I was about as
miserable as any human being possibly could be. I had no

place to turn. In football or basketball, team play usually dictates the outcome, but baseball is different—aside from the hit and run, the squeeze play, the double steal, and the double play, you're pretty much on your own. The manager can't hit for you; it's up to you as an individual to cut the mustard or get out of the way for someone who can.

One of the Dodger coaches who always had encouraged me was Pete Reiser. He's that kind of a man—enthusiastic, positive, cheerful. I went to Pete for help, and I couldn't have selected a better person. Reiser was the batting champion of the National League when he played for the 1941 Dodgers. He was affectionately called Pistol Pete because his screaming line drives to all corners of the ball park reminded Ebbets Field fans of gun shots.

So Pete took me under his wing, and we started a long series of daily sessions each afternoon in the Coliseum. We agreed to meet two hours ahead of the regular practice time. This meant Reiser would be giving up two hours of free time with his family each day, and during baseball season he didn't have too many free hours. Mindful of the sacrifices he was making, I was determined to be a model student. I knew I had a lot to learn about batting, and considered myself extremely fortunate to be tutored by one of baseball's leading experts.

We picked up a couple of clubhouse boys to shag balls and started our daily workouts. Pete made like a pitcher on the mound and I tried to look like a hitter at the plate. Most players would rather bat than eat, and normally I feel the same way. But these were not normal circumstances. I was depressed, discouraged, and my timing was definitely off.

Pete started me from scratch—almost like a manager would do with a nine-year-old Little Leaguer. He selected a new bat for me, one I could whip around faster. He opened my batting stance and worked on fundamentals such as meeting the ball out in front of the plate—taking an even swing and not overstriding. It was almost like learning a new sport. When we started out I felt I really had it made, but it wasn't that easy.

The heat, for one thing, was unbearable—a staggering 104 degrees. The floor of the Coliseum is sunken about 30 rows below ground level, and it can get like an oven down on the field.

"Man, this heat is really getting me down," I complained to Pete.

"Would you rather take a little heat here with the Dodgers or go back to the 'bus and wool-shirt circuit' in Spokane?" he asked me.

What could I say? Here was a man giving me all he had. He stood there grinning, his face wet with perspiration. It was selfish of me to have said anything other than "thanks." If it hadn't been for the lessons I learned from Pete those 13 sweltering days in the Los Angeles Coliseum, I wouldn't be in the majors today. He spent an hour and a half pitching batting practice to me, another half-hour building up my confidence. Reiser's patience, his faithful dedication to getting me back on my feet, his inspiring leadership will remain with me throughout my life.

They say in every man's life there's a guiding light—someone who believes in you, helps you over the hump, inspires you to greater heights, someone you respect and admire. My champion was Pete Reiser. Even though I had quit on myself, he never gave up on me for a moment. He was probably exhausted from the heat and exercise—after all he wasn't an active player—but I never heard him complain once. He kept driving me, spurring me on. I was ready to drop. I was emotionally and physically spent. I had been disgraced night after night in being removed for pinch hitters. I was at the end of the line.

Pete's main object was to get me to hit to the opposite field. He threw pitch after pitch while I assumed my new stance in the batter's box. He kept throwing until his arm was ready to drop off. We worked together for four days. At the end of the fourth workout I hadn't noticed any improvement in my hitting, either in practice or in the games. For the record, my average was still going down.

"Pete, we'd better call it a day. I'm wasting your time. I appreciate the help you're giving me, but I'm afraid it's no use."

Reiser didn't say a word. He went to the water cooler, took a long drink, and then suggested we take a walk to the outfield. We sat alone in this huge 100,000-seat arena. I was about to learn the power of positive thinking. Pete told me that one of the first fundamentals for success was persistence.

"No matter how tough the going gets, hang in there," he pleaded. "As corny as it sounds, always remember, *'Winners never quit and quitters never win.'* If you can learn this and practice this thinking you'll get through many a rough day—not only playing baseball but in life as well."

As I look back—how selfish can a guy get? Deep inside I wasn't selfish, I was discouraged, exhausted, whipped. But Pete never once lost faith in me. He kept driving, encouraging, coaching.

"Try to hit on top of the ball . . . just meet it . . . swing smoothly . . . choke the bat more and swing level . . . you've got the ability . . . you can hit to the opposite field . . . keep swinging . . . I'll keep throwing."

The following day we picked up the "battle," and believe me it was a real struggle. Pete didn't let up; neither did I. I gave it all I had and then some. I listened religiously, made mental notes, and finally at the end of the 13th practice we both felt I was ready to regain lost ground.

As if endowed with supernatural strength, I began hitting. My average had tumbled to .204 so I had my work cut out for me. I'm not psychic, but the way the balls started dropping for base hits made me wonder what was happening. It was like magic. My average started climbing. My entire attitude had changed from that of despair to one of eager anticipation. I couldn't wait to get up to the plate. Not only was my hitting improving but my ability on the bases had picked up as well. Up until then I only had 18 stolen bases. Taking

Reiser's advice, I took greater leads, more liberties with specific pitchers. I assumed a positive attitude toward stealing bases. This approach paid off because by the end of the season I stole 32 more for a grand total of 50—more stolen bases than any Dodger had piled up in 37 years.

Other things began to happen, too. I was elevated from the bottom of the batting order to lead-off man so the club could take advantage of my speed. Fans who had been on me were now cheering me with a chant of "Go! Go! Go!" every time I reached first base. Even the Dodger management was smiling at me as if I could do no wrong.

It was a lesson I'll never forget; it taught me that if a person wants to do something bad enough, if he really wants to succeed, he can do so if he tries. It isn't easy—worthwhile things seldom are. It takes work, sometimes days and weeks of the hardest kind of punishment, but in the long run you can look at yourself in the mirror and the reflection will be one of pride because deep in your heart you know you gave it all you had.

Did this extra effort pay off for me? I'll let you be the judge. I wound up the season with a batting average of .295 to finish among the top ten hitters in the National League.

While I've thanked him personally many times—I'd like to give Pete one more plug—this time in print. In letters ten feet high:

THANK YOU, PETE REISER, FROM THE BOTTOM
OF MY HEART.

chapter • 7

Vero Beach, U.S.A.

Spring training must cost the Dodgers a small fortune each year. Our training site, which encompasses 110 acres, is located about three miles from the city of Vero Beach, Fla., where the club has taken over a World War II Naval Air Station and remodeled and modernized it to accommodate some 400 professional baseball players.

The Dodgers also picked up the R.H.I.P. (rank has its privileges) housing system from the Navy with each major-league player quartered in the fashionable two-story annex with private room and bath, while the minor-leaguers are housed four to a room in double-deck bunks in the main barracks. This gives the players in the lower classifications an incentive to make the varsity and move to the upper echelon.

I'll never forget how anxious I was to get to spring training in 1960. I could hardly wait until I signed my contract. I'd finished the '59 season as the regular shortstop, and then we had whipped the Chicago White Sox in the World Series. All I could think about was Vero Beach and moving into the plush major-league annex. It was something I had been look-ing forward to each spring for seven years. You can imagine

my disappointment and humiliation upon registering to find
that I had been assigned to the old barracks, the same building
I'd been in each spring-training season as a minor-leaguer.
This crushed my ego. So I went over to headquarters to complain, almost with tears in my eyes. They told me not to
worry, that it shouldn't make that much difference to me.
After we discussed it awhile I decided to rise above it, bury
my pride, and remain in the barracks.

Another minor crisis occurred when I reported for infield
drills. To my amazement there were four shortstops in camp,
and each of us would have to scramble to see who would wind
up in the starting line-up. I thought my play in August and
September and in the World Series had been well above
average so I arrived at Vero Beach with the idea that I was
the Dodger shortstop, that I had the job locked up. I knew
I would have to be at my best to stay in the starting line-up, but
I expected to give my all because I've never been one to just
go through the motions. Relegation to the minor-league
quarters and the insecure feeling of not knowing I was the
No. 1 shortstop left me somewhat unnerved.

Later during that season a reporter asked me what one of
my main objectives was in baseball. I told him to go to spring
training as the Dodger shortstop and to live in the major-league
annex at Vero Beach. He thought I was joking, but at the time
I was never more serious.

The temporary demotion in 1960 made me a better ball
player. I left spring training with more determination than
ever, and finished the season with 50 stolen bases and a .295
batting average. This may be the reason the Dodgers kept me
from getting too content. They do it to other ball players, and
I was no exception. In this way they can create an impression
that each player has his work cut out for him, and also prevents
him from becoming too cocky. I'm happy to report that my
patience was rewarded. The following spring I moved into the
annex, carpets, drapes, private bath, and all. I knew then I
was really a major-leaguer.

A total of six and a half diamonds, all of them full of
Dodger players, make up the playing areas at Vero Beach. The
half diamond is for infield drills, while one of the fields is an
actual ball park known as Holman Stadium, named for Bud
Holman, one of the members of the club's board of directors.
There's a track where we run during drills and race against
each other and the stopwatch. I always was able to win these
races until Willie Davis came to camp. Other facilities include
sawdust sliding pits, batting cages with mechanical pitching
machines, and single 90-foot baselines with actual bases at
each end for practicing run-down plays.

Each day starts at 7:00 A.M. when an "official" comes
through the halls blowing a whistle and shouting, "This is
Dodgertown, let's go!" I've yet to find out who it is because
I'm still asleep at that time. After breakfast we have to be in
uniform by 9:30 A.M. or 10 depending upon the day's schedule. Players can stay in bed and skip breakfast if they prefer
as long as they're ready to play by 10. I've had no problems
getting up because the mornings are so beautiful.

The first half-hour is spent discussing activities for the day.
Then our spring-training roster of 40 to 50 players is split
up into three or four squads. This gives each player an opportunity to perform to his maximum. There's a manager or coach
in charge of each group in every diamond area.

The first or second day of spring training is devoted to pub-
licity pictures. Sandwiched in are calisthenics and laps around
the field. Once around the ball park the first time seems like
ten laps, but we soon get used to it. Bill Buhler, the Dodger
trainer, leads us in the "Happy Hour" drills, followed by more
laps and pepper games. Each day starts with calisthenics
followed by laps and specific drills.

An informal session which we go through several times each
spring involves the pitchers covering first when balls are hit
to the right side of the infield. This is one of the big plays in
baseball, and usually gets messed up a few times each season.
It can't be practiced too much.

Next we might work on timing pick-off plays. Then later we may split up again with all the outfielders going with Pete Reiser, all the pitchers with Joe Becker, and the infielders with Greg Mulleavy or another coach. Walter Alston goes from group to group watching the progress of the individual players.

All ball players like to hit so we look forward to batting practice each day. We face live pitching (which is preferable) or many times bat against the mechanical pitching machine, Iron Mike. There are eight different batting cages and eight machines. After each one is loaded, you stand in the box and hit away. You can regulate the speed of these machines to throw as hard, or even harder, than any pitcher. There's also one that can be adjusted to throw inside or outside curves. We keep one of the machines in the bull pen at Dodger Stadium and take bunting drills during pregame batting practice.

Each spring produces the usual sore arms, pulled leg muscles, and blisters. The trainers work overtime these first few weeks, then their work load eases because when it's time to break camp most of the players have rounded into playing condition. Most of the men wear golf gloves and use tincture of benzoine to prevent hand blisters. As soon as my arms and legs develop soreness three separate times, then I know I'm in shape. It's a cycle I go through each year, but after I've had my third sore arm I'm ready to play for keeps.

Ball players, like soldiers and sailors, have been known to gripe frequently, especially at mess call. However, you'll never hear complaints from any of the Dodgers over the food at Vero Beach. It's the greatest, both in quality and quantity. It's a wonder I don't gain 10 or 15 pounds each spring. Service is cafeteria style. A typical dinner includes your choice of ham, steak, chicken, roast beef, or any other entree; four or five kinds of vegetables, three or four different salads, iced tea, coffee, milk, punch, and a wide variety of desserts. Breakfast is like the *Chuck Wagon* at Las Vegas, a real truck driver's spread. Once in awhile some of the Dodger brass stand by the

line to make sure we get enough to eat. At least I guess that's
why they watch each tray so carefully as we pass by on our
way to our table.

For some unknown reason I've never had a weight problem.
I have a big appetite and enjoy my meals. Other players kid
me, warning me that I'll get fat, but they've been on this theme
for the past five years, and I still weigh the same. Some players
have to work out conscientiously during the winter months
to keep their weight down and to stay in condition. Other than
an occasional golf game, I've never exercised in between seasons. My wind is good, which it probably wouldn't be if I did
pick up extra pounds.

When spring training starts around February 27, I weigh
165. When we break camp I'm down to 163. During the
winter I may go as high as 168, but the day I leave for Vero
Beach I'm at 165 again. With calisthenics and daily workouts
I'm in midseason form within the first two weeks, leaving the
remainder of the training periods to perfect my timing.

Players who have their wives and families with them live
off the base, usually in beach homes. I would like to take
Gertrude to Vero Beach some spring. I've been there all these
years, but she has yet to set foot in Florida. I write her each
day, but her only knowledge of spring training is from my
letters. It would be more convenient if we trained in Arizona.
However, aside from my own selfish reason (and the cold
weather) I can't think of a better setup in baseball than the
fabulous training site the Dodgers have established in Vero
Beach; it's got everything.

We train about three hours each day. The rest of the day
is like time spent at a summer vacation resort. There's a
basketball court, a badminton court, tennis courts, volley ball,
a pitch and putt golf course plus a special practice green, an
Olympic-size swimming pool, shuffle board, and barbecue pits.
There's good fishing in the nearby Indian River. Indoor activities include table tennis, pool, cards, television, books, and
magazines. Every evening we have a first-run motion picture.

So if a player can't find enough to do, he's really got problems.

Some of my free time is spent fishing in the river. Many of the big fish from the Atlantic Ocean come up through the inlet where I've had excellent luck fishing off the bank. I often give the fish I catch to the chefs and maids and in turn am remembered by them with an extra blanket or two when the cold spell hits the area each spring. I spend a lot of time in my room playing the banjo which keeps the other players alert in the event they're trying to rest. One of the minor-league players, Thad Tillotson, who plays a mean guitar, has hooked up with me to grind out some torrid tunes. We hope to get a combo together some day. There's plenty of talent in the Dodger organization, and it isn't all confined to the ball field.

We'll play a number of intrasquad games, which can get pretty competitive when you realize that every man is fighting for a job. We don't knock each other down in breaking up a double play, but we play just as hard otherwise. You might find a young pitcher brushing you back after you've touched him for a couple of hits. You can't blame him. He's trying to win a job and make a livelihood. I don't try to steal too many bases. It's too easy to sprain an ankle early in the year. Another reason for not stealing too often is that it might show up a young player and hurt his chances of making the ball club.

Most of the exhibition games with other major-league clubs are played on the road. We only schedule about four or five games at Vero Beach and travel by our own private plane for about 15 other games. The longest trip is only a half-hour away. By contrast, some of the other clubs travel by bus and it often takes them from two to three hours to reach their destination.

We leave Florida and head west around eight days prior to the opening week of the season. We spend time in Phoenix playing the Giants and the Cubs, travel to Las Vegas for games with Cleveland, and may stop for games in Palm Springs with the Angels. We drew big crowds in San Diego in 1962 when

chapter · 8

"Go! Go! Go!"

BEING A FIRM believer in "what you don't know won't hurt you" I thought I had accomplished the ultimate in base stealing when I finished the 1960 season with 50 thefts. With the season well into July, I only had 18, but in the last 57 games I picked up the pace and added another 32. Unfortunately the Dodgers finished fourth, some 14 games behind. We were mathematically eliminated from the pennant when we still had two weeks to play. This is a trying time for a ball club. There's little incentive other than that of personal pride to perform up to your potential. It must be rough on ball players on second-division teams to continue to give their best every day when deep inside they know they're up a dead-end street as far as the pennant is concerned.

This is one of the reasons I set goals for myself. I think it is a good idea to have definite goals because it keeps you hustling. In '60, after I had stolen 30 bases, I was encouraged by the sportswriters, the radio announcers, my teammates and the fans to try for 40. That was my goal. To my surprise I had 40 by the middle of September. Right away I set a new mark of 50. I reached this figure the day before the season ended, so as a gesture of appreciation, the Dodger management, in a pre-game ceremony, presented me with the second-base bag to take home. At the time I didn't see how I could ever improve upon that modern Dodger record of 50 stolen bases. I had swiped 54 on successive years when I first played organized ball, but that was with a Class D club (Hornell), but this was the big time. To prove my prediction's validity, I only had 35 at the end of the '61 season, still good enough to lead the league.

When the 1962 season started, I set a goal of 50 stolen bases. This seemed a reasonable total after figuring my past performances and the fact that we would have the advantage of playing all our home games in the new ball park at Dodger Stadium. By July 27th, in our 104th game (against the San Francisco Giants) I had equaled my previous output. I didn't think about the record then; in fact, nothing was farther from my mind. For some reason I failed to set a new goal. However, on August 26th when I stole three bases in one game against the Mets to run my total to 72, I must admit the record looked like a possibility.

The same fans, writers, announcers, players and friends were no longer asking me if I thought I could break it, they were *insisting* that I do it. In fact, the enthusiasm of the fans was apparent wherever we played. It got to be commonplace for crowds in ball parks throughout the country to yell at me, "Go! Go! Go!" even though a stolen base might send their home team down to defeat.

In Los Angeles the roar of "Go! Go! Go!" was almost deafening every time I reached first base. With excitement reaching a fever pitch, I drew a parallel between my own predicament and the late spectacular bullfighter, Manolete. Encouraged by thousands of his followers, Manolete became more daring each time he entered the arena. Although he was physically exhausted, they clamored for more. They weren't satisfied with a routine performance; he had to top his previous effort. He should have quit when he was ahead, but to please the crowd he kept fighting. The law of averages finally caught up with him: he was killed.

While I wasn't facing a bull or death or even serious injury, it was easy to see how demanding fans can stimulate you and drive you to greater heights whether you're ready for it or not. It was almost like being mesmerized. The constant chanting gave me renewed strength and confidence. There were times when I didn't think I could stand, let alone run, because I was in such pain. In spite of an injured right leg, I knew I owed it to the fans to steal at every opportunity.

I also realized there would be some individuals who would be disappointed if I broke Ty Cobb's stolen-base mark of 96. There are many who speak of the good old days in reverent terms. In 1961, when Roger Maris set a new home-run total, many critics were upset because he had topped the immortal Babe Ruth. But baseball is a game of statistics, and I feel that records are meant to be broken. I'm just stubborn enough to want to break records just to prove that we modern-day ball players can do something better than the old-timers. I think it's good for baseball. You can't live in the past. I would like to see another player exceed my mark. It would be a great achievement because I know what a struggle it was for me to steal that many bases. I honestly think I would get as big a kick out of watching someone else break it as I would breaking it again myself. It is silly for players and especially fans to try to preserve records. I was proud of Bobby Doerr, former great Red Sox infielder, when I read his congratulatory comments in *The Sporting News,* after Ken Hubbs of the Chicago Cubs had surpassed his consecutive errorless-game streak. In my opinion, it's good for baseball to see new records established.

On my way to the century mark I must have broken five or six others. Some were club records, others modern-day highs. The statisticians dug deep because they came up with some men I'd never heard of, and, while it was amusing to me, my wife became quite irritated. She was pulling for me to break the record, so it gave her a great deal of satisfaction each time

I stole. Ironically, whenever I reached a new record, they'd dust off the books and find another one for me to break. This annoyed her all the more. I told her not to worry because it wasn't that important. The significant thing to me at the time was that the Dodgers were winning and everyone was well and happy.

Each day as I came closer to the record, I began to feel the tension a little more. I knew in my own heart I could break it, providing I didn't suffer any illnesses or injuries. Another concern was the possibility of a batting slump. After all, I had to reach first before I could steal second. I spent quite a few restless nights up until that record-breaking game with the Cardinals. I would lie in bed with my eyes closed. I rested, but sleep was another matter. I thought about the starting pitcher the next day, what his moves were to first, whether he violated the balk rule, how I had fared against him in the past. I thought about batting against him and how I would steal, once I reached first base. I took a mental review of previous games against him and plotted my attack.

Physically I was in pain more than half the season. One of my most serious ailments was a pulled hamstring muscle in my right leg. This was caused by sudden stops and starts. It also was hard on my legs to play on different infields. Some of the groundskeepers kept the dirt soft around first base by mixing sand with the clay. On diamonds in this condition I couldn't get enough traction as I took off. If I slipped it put an abnormal strain against my leg muscles. Spike wounds could be treated and would heal rapidly, but in September when my right leg started to bleed internally from the constant pounding, I thought I might have to leave the line-up.

It was then that the Dodger trainers, Bill Buhler and Wayne Anderson, came through like the pros that they are, to keep me on my feet. These men who had been nursing me along all season, watched me like a couple of mother hens taking care of a baby chick. They gave me all kinds of vitamins, took me in and out of the whirlpool bath, gave me diathermy treatments, massaged my feet, kept the blood circulating in my leg, and kept me running. My leg had turned an ugly purple, completely discolored from knee to hip. Just the thought of sliding on that leg sent pains through my body. Although I was taped and padded, there wasn't much one could do to protect this injury externally. At this time I started to slide headfirst on my stomach, hoping to give my leg a chance to heal. I found it hard to believe, but after two days of belly-sliding, my leg improved considerably.

I rested my leg for a few days, then slid into base the conventional way. Unfortunately, the pain returned, and I had to resume the headfirst slides. This became a pattern—one day sliding on my leg, several days on my stomach, then on my leg and back to headfirst slides again. My last 19 steals were accomplished with my leg in this condition. But I was approaching the record and to get so close and not try for it would have been something I would have regretted all my life. Every time I added another stolen base, Buhler and Anderson should have taken a bow in front of home plate because they played a big part in making it possible. We worked together like a team. As their No. 1 patient, I reported early, took special treatments, followed their instructions to the letter. I promised them I would break the record if I could steal as many as three bases in a game. They kept this in mind as they doctored me each afternoon. I know now that they gathered incentive with each stolen base and were it not for their tireless efforts the new National League mark never would have been recorded. I made a special point to tell them how much they had helped me each time I added another steal. I owe them more than I can ever repay for their devotion, kindness, and patience.

Pete Reiser also helped me increase my effectiveness on the basepaths. He was a brilliant base runner himself, and taught me many of his valuable secrets plus his positive approach, which is absolutely necessary for base-stealing success. Several times when my leg was throbbing I began feeling sorry for myself and even suggested to Pete that I rest for a day or so on the bench.

"What do you mean, your leg hurts? Get a good jump, and steal it standing up; then you don't have to slide," he joshed.

With the base-stealing record clearly visible, the most important thing of all was for the Dodgers to finish on top. I was beginning to feel the pressure as I realized that our attack had centered around my ability to get on first, steal second, and score with a hit. As we continued this method, I piled up an impressive total, and, before I was aware of it, the record was mine.

As I started closing in on Ty Cobb's mark of 96, I began to steal bases that I ordinarily wouldn't have attempted. If I hadn't taken some of these chances I never would have made it because this was no ordinary record. I remember one game in particular when we were playing the Mets in the Polo Grounds on August 26th. We were leading, 12-4, and by the seventh inning I had added three bases to run my total to 72. I asked Walter Alston to take me out, knowing it was a good chance to rest. When he did, the New York fans nearly booed him out of the park. They were screaming for me to steal more bases. (I learned later that I should have listened to them.) I didn't want to keep embarrassing the pitchers; on the other hand, I knew I had to keep charging after the record.

On September 7th against the Pittsburgh Pirates I had my best base-stealing game of the season. I stole four, giving me 82, and setting a new National League mark. The old mark of 80 had been posted by Bob Bescher of Cincinnati in 1911.

The following telegram was waiting for me at Dodger Stadium the next day:

NATIONAL LEAGUE OF PROFESSIONAL BASEBALL CLUBS
SEPT. 8, 1962

MR. MAURY WILLS
LOS ANGELES DODGERS
c/o DODGER STADIUM

1000 ELYSIAN PARK AVE.
LOS ANGELES, CALIF.

MY SINCERE CONGRATULATIONS BOTH PERSONALLY AND
ON BEHALF OF OUR LEAGUE. BREAKING A NATIONAL
LEAGUE BASE STEALING RECORD WHICH HAS PREVAILED
SO LONG IS A GREAT ACHIEVEMENT AND WE ARE PROUD
TO HAVE GREAT YOUNG BALL PLAYERS SUCH AS YOU HOLD
THESE RECORDS. NOW GO ALL THE WAY AND BREAK THE
RECORD HELD BY THE GREAT TY COBB.

WARREN C. GILES
PRESIDENT

I sent him the following air-mail letter in answer to his telegram which I appreciated very much:

LOS ANGELES DODGERS
DODGER STADIUM
1000 ELYSIAN PARK AVE.
LOS ANGELES, CALIF.
September 11, 1962

Mr. Warren C. Giles
President
National Baseball League
Carew Tower
Cincinnati, Ohio

Dear Mr. Giles:

I want to thank you sincerely for your wire. I am very happy to have been able to contribute a record for the National League and hope I can carry on to an even greater record before the season is completed.

Your wire was very inspiring.

Sincerely,

Maury Wills

Two weeks later we blew into St. Louis to face the Cards in

the first of a three-game series. I needed three more stolen bases to set a new record. This didn't seem difficult; I had three games to do it.

You can imagine my disappointment when I learned that Baseball Commissioner Ford Frick had ruled I must steal three bases in the 154th game the next night to break Cobb's mark. It was a rough ruling to accept. All I could think of was another 15 bases I could have stolen but didn't because I had two or three and didn't want to make the other clubs angry. When Cobb set his record in 1915 he did so in 156 games. There were two extra games played because of ties. Ironically, Cobb stole two of his 96 bases during one of these replays. I had been under the impression that I had 156 games, not 154 as Frick had ruled. Had I known earlier, I could have tried for five or six extra thefts before this game. I know I could have had a few more because I was only thrown out 13 times during the entire season.

In game No. 154 I stole only one base. It was a result of a walk, the only time I reached first. Then on September 23rd, in our 156th game, I stole two more to establish a new major-league record of 97. Following the game, the Cards graciously presented me with the second-base bag. I thought this was a wonderful display of sportsmanship on their part. I'm planning to give the base to the Baseball Hall of Fame in Cooperstown, N.Y.

While all this base stealing was going on we were in a bitter battle to maintain our National League lead. We were barely out in front of the Giants and fighting every inch of the way. I stole No. 96 when we were trailing by one run. This is against the book which says play it safe when you're behind. I don't think you should always play the game by the book, because, like in many other successful ventures, you have to gamble now and then. In playing to win there's always an element of risk, and unless you make a few unconventional decisions you're apt to wind up third or fourth or maybe in the second division.

Rather than go by the book, you've got to play your hunches. It often crosses up the other team; it's good strategy to keep them guessing. That's the way I've tried to play, and this is one reason I've been able to steal successfully (bases, that is!).

I felt the pressure. I had to weigh carefully each steal attempt. I had to make sure I got a good jump. The last thing I wanted to do was to abuse the privilege of running on my own. Walter Alston knew I was feeling the strain and that I first was concerned with the Dodgers' winning. I'll never forget this particular game in St. Louis when we were behind and I still needed two to break the record.

"If you get on, little man, take second," he ordered. I couldn't get over it. Here was a man trying to win the game, as well as the pennant, and yet he was kind enough to place my own personal importance on the same plane with the entire ball club. He really went out of his way to help me. I have to thank him twice: (1) for letting me bat in the lead-off position; and (2) for giving me the opportunity to run on my own. By showing confidence in me, he helped me build up my own self-assurance so that I could be successful in my base-stealing attempts.

Another player who owns a piece of the new stolen-base mark is Jim Gilliam. His role in the No. 2 position in our batting order was one of the keys to my success. I told Jim at the beginning of the season not to take any unnecessary pitches, not to do anything that would endanger his own personal record to help me steal bases. It's important for each individual player to have a good year. Even if his team wins the pennant, if a player has a bad year he can't expect a raise. Raises are almost always issued on individual performances alone. I know Jim sacrificed his own personal gains many times to help me. I can't think of another player in baseball better suited to follow me in the batting order. He isn't a first-ball hitter and doesn't jump around going for bad pitches. Before a pitcher finishes with him, usually he has had to throw five or six pitches, and that's all I need to pull a steal.

Sid Ziff, veteran sportswriter for the Los Angeles Times, who has been one of my biggest fans, had this comment in his column in August 1962:

GILLIAM'S PATIENCE HELPS WILLS

Batting behind Wills, Jim Gilliam has made a definite contribution to Maury's success. If he was an impatient batter and swung at everything, Maury wouldn't have much chance to steal.

Gilliam often has held back to give Maury a chance, Jim told me. "But that's part of the game," he said, refusing to take any credit for it.

"We're better off if he's on second and in scoring position. That's only playing to win.

"Sure, I have laid off the ball intentionally. Sometimes the ball will be right down the middle, too. But I'm in no hurry to hit. You only hit but one pitch and I'm in no hurry."

Gilliam makes the ideal type to be hitting behind Wills. And it hasn't hurt him any, either. He's enjoying a big year and hitting .284. "But don't be giving me any credit," says Jim. "You gotta give him ALL the credit because he's doing the running. Don't you be giving me credit."

Jim isn't a pull hitter. The infield can't cheat toward right field. He is a spray hitter, and it's impossible to play him in any specific manner. This gives me a great advantage in keeping the shortstop and the second baseman honest. They can't cover the base because they don't know which direction to favor in going after the ball. Just by his being Jim Gilliam, that's the way he's helped me the most!

Last and most important are the fans. But for them there wouldn't be professional baseball. They were just great both at home and in all other nine ball parks—yes, even Candlestick Park in San Francisco. The crescendo which built up to an ear-splitting roar every time I reached first base in Dodger

Stadium is something I'll never forget. I couldn't begin to measure the genuine warmth I felt inside each time they shouted "Go! Go! Go!" At times like these I forgot my injured leg and ran with only one thought in mind—to steal the base. It was the support from the fans that inspired me to get a good jump, to try for the record, to succeed because this was what they wanted me to do. I owe them a great vote of appreciation and thanks for the confidence they showed in me right up through the final play-off game with the Giants.

Oddly enough, one of my best games of the 1962 season was in the last game of the year against San Francisco. I stole my 102nd base the first time I got on. Then in the seventh with Juan Marichal pitching, I stole second, then third, and when the throw bounced past Jim Davenport, I came home to give us what appeared to be a safe 4-2 lead. (We lost 6-4.) This gave me a season high of 104 stolen bases. I also went four-for-five that day and wound up with 208 base hits, the most registered by a National League shortstop since Dave Bancroft set the record with 209 back in 1922. Ironically, I missed another record by one—the most times at bat in a single season. One record I'm proud of is that in playing in every game of the season (165), it was the highest number of games in history for an individual player in a single year. The National League expansion and the three play-off games made this possible.

A personal mark which I missed by one percentage point was my final batting average of .299. I had set .300 as a goal and had I collected a hit my last time at bat I would have made it.

Do I think I'll ever steal 104 bases again? No, I can't believe I did it to this day. I don't see how I can ever come close again. The physical beating I took is more than I want to endure. I still like to run, want to run, and plan to run, especially if it will help the ball club. If we need a stolen base, I'll definitely try to steal it. That's the same idea I had at the beginning of the 1962 season, and before I knew it the record was in sight. If I pile up another impressive total the fans might want me to go for a new record, but at the moment I don't see how it can happen.

It's difficult to predict the future. It's something that pretty well takes care of itself. I don't expect to have another year like I had in '62, but stranger things have happened. One thing is certain: I'm going to have to get on base. My 208 hits plus walks and errors gave me an opportunity to steal that I might not receive again. And no matter how they kid about it, first base is one bag you can't steal. I've tried it; it can't be done! This was the first time in my career that I discovered that crime doesn't pay.

chapter • 9

Formula for Success

THERE'S ONE AMAZING thing about professional baseball: if you're a fanatic, the season never ends. The hot-stove league continues throughout the winter with debate extending across the country from Burt Ketcham's Hardware Store in Lyndonville, Vt., to Bob Misrach's United Sporting Goods Center in Los Angeles. During these heated off-season sessions almost every inning of every key game is played and replayed a hundred times or more.

We were booting around a few opinions ourselves one winter afternoon in Don Odessky's office on La Cienega Boulevard in Beverly Hills, listing what a ball player must have to make it in the majors. Don has represented me in several of my business ventures including my record promotions, and is one of the bigger Dodger boosters in the West. One subject we tried to clarify was whether a player could make good through applying a formula for success, or because he was born with great natural ability.

"What tools do you think a player needs to be a successful major leaguer?" Odessky asked me.

"Leo Durocher says a man needs only to master five basic

fundamentals to reach the top in the big leagues," I responded.
"Leo claims a player must be able to run, throw, field, hit, and
hit with power. Other helpful traits are desire, proper attitude,
enthusiasm, concentration, relaxation, aptitude, good eyesight,
a competitive spirit, courage, and a sense of timing."

It sounds simple, but each of these abilities is a demanding
one. If you go through each major-league roster you won't
find too many players who are outstanding in all these departments. You'd have to name players the caliber of Mickey
Mantle, Willie Mays, Ernie Banks, Roger Maris, Tommy
Davis, and Henry Aaron. If a man is a power hitter, he may
lack running speed. Another player might be able to field and
throw but have trouble getting his batting average over .250.
The complete ball player, as the sportswriters describe him, is
almost an imaginary person.

Before a baseball player can even put on a uniform he must
have an abundance of natural ability. He has to be able to run
—preferably faster than the average athlete. He must be able
to throw accurately and with conviction. He must have good
eyesight in order to follow the ball from the split second the
pitcher releases it right up to the instant he hits it. Scouts
claim that if you can run and throw—if you stand out in these
departments which are God-given—they can teach you the
fundamentals of fielding and hitting.

The ability to throw is something that can't be taught although you can strengthen and develop your arm with special
exercises. I try to practice my accuracy during infield drills
especially on off-balance throws to second and first. My experience as a pitcher helped me throw accurately when I was converted to an infielder.

Running, like throwing, is something you inherit. You can
be a better base runner with practice. There are tricks to any
trade, including baseball. With proper instruction and concentration, a player can get a faster jump on the pitcher, can
start beating out infield hits, and cover more ground in the
field. It's up to the individual to determine how far he wants

to go to strive for perfection. Stamina and endurance are important physical tools that can be acquired. They say when a player starts to slip, his legs are the first to go; I'll be able to verify that statement in a few more years.

To be consistently successful in baseball a player must get in condition and stay in condition. Baseball doesn't beat you up physically like football does. You receive cuts, bruises, spike wounds, sprains, and other assorted injuries, but there's very little body contact. As a result there's no excuse for not being in the best of shape at all times. Babe Ruth played in another era, but the tales they tell about his consumption of hot dogs, beer, candy, and peanuts have become legendary. Writers have tabbed Ruth as the greatest. Would he have been even greater had he kept in better condition? You have to believe he could have run faster if nothing else.

Al Buffington, Hollywood advertising executive, questioned the importance of quick reflexes. A player with fast hands may come by this naturally or he can develop this skill with practice. Quick reflexes, especially for catchers and infielders, are most desirable. It's important to react quickly when batting— to get out of the way of a pitch or to cross up the infield by laying down a bunt. I developed faster hand and body reflexes by throwing a tennis ball against a wall. Some players find that handball serves the same purpose. Pepper games also keep a player on his toes.

All things being equal, as far as physical ability is concerned, the player who exhibits the most courage is the one I'd want on my team. There never has been a champion who wasn't courageous. It takes a special kind of fortitude to hit with men on base. Some players choke up; they can't stand pressure. It requires another type of guts to stand still in the batter's box when a wild fast-baller is burning pitches around your head at speeds just under 100 miles an hour. It takes courage to get in front of screaming ground balls that can snap your jaw bone or break your nose should you get hit, but fear doesn't belong in baseball. I take the attitude that it's just a baseball and that

if I get hit it's only going to hurt for a little while. I've had
my share of bad hops. I've been hit in the head, the eye, the
cheek, and on various parts of my body. But the pain was
temporary, and I tried not to let it interfere with my play.
Once a player becomes gun shy he starts letting the ball play
him. That's bad. He must play the ball if he expects to be
a good infielder.

Scouts always are looking for prospects with natural batting
ability. A man with a relaxed, level swing who can power the
ball attracts their attention. This is a technique which can
be taught providing the physical ability is there in the beginning. Many managers won't tamper with a player's batting
style, especially if he's maintaining a good average. If a player
is in a slump or obviously needs help, it's there waiting for
him. Bobby Bragan helped me increase my average by teach-
ing me to switch hit. Then in 1960, when I hit my big slump,
Pete Reiser brought me back up again with his expert advice.

Cardinal Stan Musial is a living example of why managers
don't like to convert awkward-looking batters. Scouts and fans
laughed when Stan crouched at the plate. Twenty years later
they were still laughing—not at Stan but at themselves for
their prediction that Musial would never be a batting success
because of his peculiar crouch. Musial went on to rewrite
most of the National League batting records, and you will find
him listed as one of the top outfielders in baseball annals.
Another star with an unorthodox stance was Gil McDougald,
ex-Yankee infielder. Gil stood with his left foot in the bucket,
but he was a real clutch player with his timely hitting.

Proper attitude is another splendid asset a player can develop. If he's open-minded and wants to learn, he can improve
in a dozen different ways. There are wise guys in baseball as
there are in other professions. The longer I've been in the
game, the more I've learned. You have to have a dedicated
attitude if you want to be a star. You must have desire. You
have to give up many pleasures and social obligations. You'll
also make certain sacrifices. A player seeking success has to go

Wills shows the form that enabled him to steal 104 bases in 1962, break Ty Cobb's 47-year-old record, and win the National League's Most Valuable Player Award, the Associated Press Athlete of the Year Award, and the *Sporting News* Major League Player of the Year Award.

Lee Balterman, Sport Magazine

Playing for Leon in winter league baseball in Mexico in 1953, Wills scores against catcher Bimbo Villegas.

1951—during his first year of professional baseball with the Hornell, N. Y. club of the Class "D" Pony League. Wills played second base, hit .280, and stole 54 bases.

Maury Wills and Ike, his German shorthair hunting dog, on a trip through "Inland Empire," of which Spokane, Washington is the hub. The Chamber of Commerce of Spokane, Wills' adopted home town, named him the city's outstanding citizen in October, 1962.

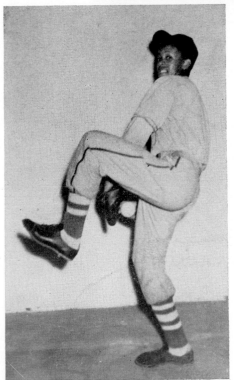

Maury "Sonny" Wills as an all-star school pitcher for Cardozo H. S., Washington, D.C., '47. Wills averaged 15-18 strikeouts per game and posted a 25-2 record.

Maury Wills, who plays the guitar and banjo and sings, formed a night-club act with some of his Dodger teammates at the close of the 1962 season. (L. to R.) Duke Snider, Wills, Frank Howard, Sandy Koufax, Don Drysdale, Willie Davis. The group appeared on stage in Las Vegas with Milton Berle.

that extra mile. This is true in anything you do, and it's paid dividends for me in baseball.

While it's normal for a player to be tense before a game, it's also imperative that he relax once the umpire shouts "Play ball." Relaxation comes from experience and confidence. When an infielder knows he has the ability to field his position, to make the right play at the right time, he has no problems. During every infield drill I work to improve my throws. I react as I would under game conditions, making each play an important one. This is valuable experience because these plays which might seem difficult at first become routine with practice. Batting practice sharpens your timing. After you've collected a few hits you gain confidence. This is in contrast to the player in a slump who starts pressing, tightens up, and starts swinging at bad balls. Talk is cheap. You can tell a player to relax, but, like thinking, it's something he has to do himself.

A player with an aptitude for baseball also is sought by scouts. They like to work with youngsters who learn rapidly. Some players are so absorbed in the game they pick up pointers in a few days that others take weeks to learn. The man who can think clearly and quickly is a valuable addition to any team. An intelligent player continually studies the opposition. He knows their strong and weak points at bat and in the field. He knows whether he can take another base on the right fielder, if he can steal on the pitcher, if the catcher has a strong arm. He knows how to play the No. 3 man in the batting order because he may hit a lot of balls up the middle. When two teams are evenly matched, this knowledge can make the difference between victory and defeat.

A successful player must realize his own limitations. He has to make adjustments in his hitting to get on base the best way he can. Perhaps he'll drag a bunt, or try to hit a high hopper, or bounce one through a hole in the infield. The big guy can grab the bat by the knob and go for the long ball. There's no defense for the home run so the man with power is much in demand. The next time one joins the Dodgers we'll find a place for him; there's always room for one more slugger.

One of the great stars I admired and considered a real champion was Bob Feller. I only saw him play once, but in that brief time he showed me a lot of class. He was on the field before the game taking exercises, stretching and strengthening his muscles. He wasn't going through the motions just to limber up; he had a definite training program which he followed. He was practicing self-discipline. Coaches can teach you so much; there's a limit to the amount you can gather from a lecture. The rest depends on you and how far you want to advance. Feller was a great example to me. When he was in the dugout he was developing his grip, his fingers, and his wrists by squeezing a rubber ball. No one told him to do this. He did it on his own. He was one of the leading pitchers in the American League and was striking out more than 200 batters a season, so it was difficult to see how he could get any better. Yet he wasn't satisfied merely to be a winning pitcher; he sought perfection. Feller was a gentleman and a great credit to the game. I was pleased when he made the Hall of Fame in 1962.

You'll hear fans say a team was lucky, that it got the breaks. I don't take too much stock in good or bad luck; I think you make your own breaks. In football if there's a fumble, the ball carrier probably was hit so hard that the ball was jarred loose. The defending team—if it recovered the ball—made its own break. Pitchers have lost games when giving up only one hit, yet that hit scored a runner who had walked.

I remember watching the Yankee-Pirate World Series on TV and thinking how Tony Kubek must have felt when that ball took a bad hop and hit him in the neck. It was a bad break for the Yankees, but a lucky one for Pittsburgh. If the hitter had popped up, struck out, or fouled out, this key play wouldn't have happened, and the Yanks might have won. The fact that Bill Virdon was able to get good wood on the ball was a tribute to his ability to come through under pressure.

Baseball is a highly competitive sport in that it offers each player an enormous challenge. Regardless of how well you play, you can almost always play better.

Through the years the Dodgers have had their share of fierce competitors. Pete Reiser was one of them. His feat of stealing home seven times in one season (1946) is an all-time National League record that he is hoping I'll surpass. In addition, Reiser practically demolished the outfield fences at Ebbets Field as he crashed into them in pursuit of line drives and fly balls. And who will ever forget Jackie Robinson's clutch hitting, daring base running, and fighting spirit? I would say that Don Drysdale is one of the strongest competitors on our present ball club. When the going gets rough, Don is at his best. He is a hard loser, and that's the way it should be. As the late Red Sanders, successful football coach at U.C.L.A, remarked one day, "Winning isn't everything, it's the only thing!"

When things go wrong and you lose you don't have to like it, but you might as well accept it. Perhaps you as an individual were the goat of the game. I've thrown wildly to first, permitting runs to score, other times I've struck out in the ninth with the bases loaded with our team one run behind. It's normal to be a hard loser, but there's no use brooding over it. Next time out you've got a chance to apply the pressure to the other team. Fortunately, in baseball, there's always another game to be played. There's always another season. This we learned the hard way one smoggy October day back in 1962.

My concept of luck is that God takes care of those who look out for themselves. Some people said I was lucky when I was called up to the Dodgers, that I was lucky to be in the majors. I like to think I was fortunate. I feel it was God's will and that I was in the right place at the right time. When the opportunity came I was ready. I made the break myself. I learned to switch hit, I did everything my minor-league manager Bobby Bragan told me to do and more. I had a great desire to succeed. I became a dedicated base runner and infielder. I persisted in my ambition to become a big leaguer. There's a proven formula for success which is known as your "ABC's." "A" is for *ability*—you must have that no matter what you do. "B" is for *breaks*—the opportunity to use your ability. "C" is for *courage*—courage to accept the challenge to use your ability to capitalize on the break that was offered you.

chapter · 10

How to Steal

THERE ARE so many factors involved in stealing a record number of bases that I couldn't begin to list them. I still can't believe I did it. It seems incredible. But the record is there in black and white, big as life for everyone to see. I'm mighty proud to be the new base-stealing champion.

As mentioned elsewhere, I wouldn't have reached this mark were it not for certain individuals and the fact that I had an exceptionally good (for me) hitting year. Batting in the lead-off position, being able to steal on my own, having Jim Gilliam hitting behind me in the batting order, playing in a spacious new ball park, getting encouragement from Pete Reiser and Walt Alston, taking medical care from Bill Buhler and Wayne Anderson, positive thinking, and moral support from 2½ million Dodger Stadium fans all contributed to my success.

In 1961, I got off to a miserable start and by August 9 had only 21 thefts. I added a few more but ended the season with only 35. A newspaper column quoted Walt Alston as saying the pitchers were the ones to blame. "The only thing holding Maury back is the pitchers. They are cheating by not coming to a stop. Warren Giles (National League president) sent out a bulletin about them not stopping, but it hasn't done any good. Last year Wills stole 50 bases and was thrown out only 12 times. This year he's stolen 21 bases and has been caught 11 times. If the cheating becomes much more flagrant next years as it has this, there won't be any stolen bases at all," Alston remarked.

The umpires did enforce the balk rule, and if they continue this practice I'll be able to continue my larceny. The rule states that a pitcher must remain in a set position for a complete second. I reached second several times in '62 because the pitchers balked.

Without giving away all of my trade secrets, it might be interesting to disclose some of the routines I followed in piling up my record. First, I watch the pitcher closely from the dugout. I study his moves to the plate when he has men on base. If I've faced him before, I know what liberties I can take against him once I get on base. I've never had to keep written notes, just mental ones. As I move into the on-deck circle I study the game situation to see if it is practical for me to steal if and when I do get to first.

The catcher is important, too, but he can have the greatest arm in baseball and it won't do him a bit of good if the pitcher doesn't hold me on or prevent me from getting a jump on him.

Each pitcher handles himself differently with men on base. I watch his feet, his hands and arms, his shoulders, and his head. He may not know it, but he usually does something different when he intends to throw to the plate rather than first. When he telegraphs his intention I start for second. Probably statisticians will go through the box scores to list the pitchers who permitted me the most number of stolen bases in 1962. I hope this list isn't published because they might change their habits and I won't be able to take the same liberties in the future.

One of the indications that the ball will be thrown to the plate (instead of first) is when a pitcher stands with an open shoulder. When he's ready to throw toward home, his shoulder is usually on a line to the plate; if he wants to pick me off, he usually turns more toward first. If he commits himself with a move toward the batter he has to throw home or a balk is called. As soon as I see him start the pitch, I'm off and running.

Some pitchers kick high when they are going for the plate, and this is another sign I watch for when I reach first. Other pitchers will move their head in a certain way. This move also gives me a good headstart.

Larry Jackson of the Cardinals, Warren Spahn of the Braves, and ex-Dodger Roger Craig now of the Mets are pitchers who cause me the most trouble. Craig will throw to first six or eight times in an effortless motion. He's perfected his pick-off throws, and were he not a former teammate I might get angry with him for trying to keep me bottled up. There are some pitchers who don't like to throw to first. They feel they might throw the ball away and give me an extra base. You can afford a bigger lead on them, and naturally they are easier to steal on than guys like Craig who you know will keep you alert.

While I never played with Jackie Robinson (he retired in 1957) I understand that he used to give the opposing pitchers fits. He was low-bridged frequently as they tried to get even with him. But Jackie was a different type of player than I am. He weighed around 200 pounds, and he could hold his own in a fight. I can see me clashing with a giant like Gene Conley who stands six feet eight inches. He'd be able to pick me up with one hand and whack me around with the other. Of course, he'd have to catch me first.

I like everyone. I want to be friends with all, especially the pitchers. If they start throwing at my legs, I'm dead. I have enough trouble with pulled muscles and spike wounds not to incur any other injuries. Some pitchers have thrown at my legs, but in doing so balls have ricocheted off my shins and I've reached base and then scored.

Another decision I must make once I arrive at first is

whether to steal. It depends a lot on the game situation and the score. For example, if we're behind three or four runs and it's late in the game, I won't accomplish much by stealing second because even If I did eventually score we'd still be more than one run behind. And should I be thrown out, this could kill a rally. If I'm the lead-off batter in the first inning or if it's a tie game, then my presence on second is much more significant, and I can usually score on any ball hit through the infield.

Sometimes I steal on the first pitch. Again it depends on the pitcher and his motion to first. I try to guess what type of pitch I'd throw under the same circumstances and govern myself accordingly. A lot of pitchers throw sliders and slow-breaking stuff which not only take a split second longer to reach the plate, but often are difficult for the catcher to handle because they pull him out of position. I've been able to steal on pitchouts, but only because I knew the pitcher wasn't going to try and pick me off.

A good lead, of course, is important. Fred Haney, general manager of the Angels and ex-teammate of Ty Cobb (and himself a fine base runner in his day) claims that Cobb got a longer lead and a quicker jump than I did, but that I could outrun him on a straightaway. Some hurlers will let you take a fair lead, but just when you think they're going for home they'll fire the ball over to first. You have to experiment on a trial-and-error basis until you know how far you can go before he'll turn and throw. A good lead is one of the fundamentals in base stealing, but I try not to overextend myself so that I'll get picked off.

I always remember to keep my body moving. You can get away faster when you're in motion rather than standing still. Once a pitcher keeps you flat-footed he enjoys an advantage. I shuffle back and forth, bend my knees, try to keep my weight on the balls of my feet. When the pitcher starts for the plate I start for second. I pivot on my right foot and cross over with my left. I'm immediately in high gear, which is absolutely necessary. Even with average speed, a player can steal a lot of bases by getting a good lead and a good jump on the pitcher.

The instant I start for second I can tell if the play is going to be close. It's something I've picked up from experience. After several years in baseball I can calculate the time it takes for the ball to reach the catcher, for the catcher to step and throw to second, and how long it's going to take me to reach the base. A lot depends on my lead and whether I get a good jump. As I come in I usually can tell where the ball is going by watching the man covering the base. I try to keep an eye on the ball as I start my slide. Occasionally the ball goes through in the outfield, so if I can get to my feet fast enough I can make it to third.

One basic thing I've mastered in stealing bases is to slide late. I stay on my feet longer than most players. This helps me two ways: I get to the base quicker, and I can twist my body to avoid being tagged.

Unlike many base runners who bend their left leg as they slide, I go in with my legs extended, making a "V." If you bend your leg you have to take another three feet and that often is the difference between being out or safe. With my legs straight I travel the shortest distance possible, 90 feet, minus my heel. I move to the right with my right leg and upper body and hit the outer edge of the bag with my left foot. I twist the rest of my body from my hips trying to avoid the defensive man. If possible the only thing I give him to tag is my feet. This "snake slide," as Casey Stengel calls it, enables me to slip under throws that are only two feet off the ground.

This is my conventional way of sliding. When I pulled the muscles in my right leg toward the end of the '62 season I had to go in on my stomach from necessity. While I stole several bases this way I wouldn't want to do it indefinitely. It's too hard on your ribs.

Base stealing for me is another sport all by itself. It's a game within a game. I'm the mouse and the cats are trying to trap me. I try to outguess the pitcher as to what pitch he'll throw. I've been fortunate in this respect, stealing many times on hunches alone. It could be instinct or a sixth sense. Whatever it is, I hope it stays with me for a few more years.

For some base stealers the pitchout often cuts them down, causing them to lose confidence. I've never given it too much thought. Once I take off for second, I'm long gone. Sometimes it's tougher for a catcher to handle a pitchout than a regular fast ball down the middle. I've stolen quite a few bases on pitchouts so they really haven't curbed my efforts too effectively.

One of the real secrets of my success in stealing is positive thinking, which I acquired from Pete Reiser. Pete has kept after me ever since I joined the club to think positive in everything I do. Like batting, stealing bases is a matter of confidence. When I'm in this frame of mind, I not only think, I *know,* I can beat the throws of the pitcher and the catcher. My efforts in 1962 proved I was right most of the time. Out of 117 attempts, I was caught only 13 times. According to the record, Cobb was thrown out 38 times during his big season in 1915.

When I take too long a lead, the pitcher tries to force me back to first. If I were a negative thinker, I'd be back hugging the bag. But after each toss I take a new lead as if the previous throw hadn't been made. You can't be on the defensive. Once a pitcher has you worried, you'll unknowingly give ground and this can cost you a theft. In thinking positively, I know I'm going to get a good lead, a good jump, and be successful even if the ball beats me to the bag.

You can't be a good base runner and practice safety first. You've got to take chances. You can't be careless, but you have to be daring. My success in base running is attributed to the fact that I've completely eliminated the fear of failure. Once you erase any doubt that you might get caught you immediately become a better base runner. With doubt you can decrease your chances at least 50 per cent.

Whenever I get on base against a pitcher who is sharp on

the pick-off play, or at holding the runner close to the base, or even in facing an infield combination that attempts a lot of pick-offs, I take a positive approach. I try to match my wits and ability against theirs, and feel that I can come out on top. I think the base runner has an advantage because the pitcher has to commit himself first.

Several infielders in the National League like to play close to the base and hold the runners on; if the second baseman or shortstop does this, then a bigger hole is opened up in the infield for the hitter. Other men don't like to leave their defensive position to fool around with the runner. This helps me because I can take a longer lead and have a better chance of stealing the base. If I'm off of second, a good lead can mean a run on a ball that is hit through the infield.

Jose Pagan, the Giants' shortstop, fiddles around a lot in back of second base trying to chase you back to the bag. He's even running you back when the pitcher is squeezing the resin bag. He leaves the hole open between third and short, but always seems to be in position when the ball is delivered. I would imagine he's a pretty tired boy by the time the game is ended. He can get away with it in San Francisco where it's always cool, but if he were in Philadelphia, St. Louis, or Cincinnati he'd be worn out by midseason with all that running.

Many experts claim that stealing third is easier than stealing second. I agree because you only steal third when you are almost certain you can make it. When you try for second, it's more of a gamble. If you can run at all you're considered in scoring position when you're on second. You can score on a base hit. It's bad baseball to get thrown out trying to steal third. Although there are nine or ten more ways you can score from third than you can from second, you can't afford to be thrown out many times going into third. I stole third 16 times during 1962 and was out only once. If they start nipping me at third, Walt Alston will start controlling me, so I have to be alert. Before I steal third, I'm 90 per cent positive that I can get the job done. I'm almost halfway there before the pitcher releases the ball. It's a matter of timing and depends a lot on the individual pitcher. A left-hander is usually easier to steal third off because his back is toward you, and you can get a better jump.

In stealing I always try to get in a direct line with the two bases. About the only time I'm not in a direct line is in Candlestick Park when the ground is wet. Then I have to wade around until I can find a possible dry spot.

I know when I take off for third there are some catchers who would rather hold the ball and give me the base without a play. Several of them are afraid the ball will go through to left field. But they would look bad if they didn't make some effort to catch me, so they throw. This happened in the final game of the season when I stole second, then third, and came home when Ed Bailey threw the ball past Jim Davenport.

As for stealing home, this is a different story altogether. Pete Reiser, who holds the league record of seven thefts in one season, has been working on me to try it more often. Leo Durocher also has needled me to chance it. It seems like every time I make up my mind to steal home I look toward the plate and there's big Frank Howard. So if there's less than two outs it's foolish to risk it when I can score on most any kind of a hit. With Howard up, and Tommy Davis, the league's leading hitter and RBI king, on deck, there doesn't seem to be any percentage in trying to get home without help.

My future success as a base stealer is somewhat unpredictable. One thing is certain: the pitchers will be out to get me. They'll be thinking of ways to slow me down or stop me. Meanwhile, if the fans will just continue to holler "Go! Go! Go!," I'll continue to run, run, run.

chapter • 11

"Let the Boys
Have Fun"

HIGH ON THE list of controversial activities for boys today is Little League baseball. I've read complaints against it in magazine articles; I've also talked with parents, Little Leaguers themselves, and their managers. Some of the criticism is justified; some is not. One thing I've learned, however, is whether you're for or against it—like a mother-in-law—it's here to stay. Personally I'm in favor of the program, with a few reservations. I feel it gives boys an opportunity to learn a difficult sport at an early age. It exposes them to a game that can hold their interest and provide them with endless enjoyment throughout their lives. Baseball is America—a game that teaches sportsmanship, one that seeks excellence of performance, and requires split-second decisions. It also teaches its participants to think. Baseball is wholesome and it's manly. There's no room for cowards or cheaters.

From what I've gathered, the major objection to the Little League program is the strong emphasis placed on winning. Everyone wants to win—the players, the parents, the managers. But in a baseball game with two teams involved there's always a winner and always a loser—even tie games eventually

91

are played off. I've heard that most of the pressure to win comes from the managers. When they can field a winner, they not only satisfy their own egos but in many cases are looking hopefully toward all-star competition, as they picture themselves managing a team in the Little League World Series in Williamsport, Pa.

Some managers require their teams to practice long hours two and three times a week. There's so much regimentation that the game ceases to be fun as far as the boys are concerned. Managers and parents often expect too much. It amazes me that most of them play as well as they do, especially with so much abnormal pressure on them. Many boys aren't ready to take on the added responsibility that baseball demands, others don't have the aptitude or the inclination.

Steve Gardner, my copilot on this book, who has been a Little League manager in Westwood (Calif.) for the past six years, told me about a father who monetarily encouraged his son to get hits. The boy would get a dollar for every home run he hit, 50 cents for a double, and a quarter for every single. This to me is ridiculous. It defeats the purpose of the sport and distorts competitive aspects of the program.

Fred Haney, one of the top executives in organized baseball, passed on some sound advice to Little League managers and coaches at a clinic a few years ago. Mr. Haney, himself a former big leaguer, managed the St. Louis Browns, the Pittsburgh Pirates, and the 1957 Milwaukee Braves, who defeated the New York Yankees in the World Series. When he talks about baseball he does so with authority.

"Don't try to teach the kids to swing the way you did; don't teach them to slide the way you did; don't teach them to throw the way you did. No matter how hard you try, they'll never be able to play just like you did," he quipped. "The main thing for you managers to remember is to *let the boys have fun*. The kids are only young once; they grow up awfully fast. They'll get plenty of specialized coaching when they get into high school. They'll probably be ready for it then. Right now it isn't too important whether you field a winning team or not. Keep your sense of humor, have a good time, turn the kids loose."

My advice to a boy starting out to play Little League ball is to select a bat he can handle, one that isn't too heavy and that he can swing with ease. Most Little League bats are made by Hillerich & Bradsby, the same firm that makes the Louisville Sluggers that we use in the major-leagues. The bats are scale models, reduced proportionately in size, weight, and length. Pick out a bat that isn't too long, choke it an inch or more, and don't try for the long ball. If in time you turn out to be a big, strong, husky kid, then you can take a harder cut. At first, however, it's best just to meet the ball, to swing evenly. It's important to be comfortable, relaxed, to concentrate on hitting the ball. Try to develop good habits, to learn proper fundamentals. Try to perfect your natural ability. When you get into your teens you can strive for more advanced skills and techniques.

Any boy interested in improving his play should see as many major-league games as possible. If he can't attend in person, he may have an opportunity to watch the games on television. Watch all the players to see how each performs. Don't focus all your attention on one particular player. Try to learn the assignments of each player because you might be playing any one of nine positions as you get older. You can be a pitcher one year and an outfielder the next. Sooner or later the coaches and managers will decide where your talents can best serve the team, and that's where you'll play.

Whether you are in Little League, Pony League, or the Sally League, when you first step out on the diamond, make your practice sessions mean something. Have an objective in mind, a definite reason for throwing the ball a certain way, for running the bases in a specific pattern. If you're supposed to circle the bases after your last swing in the batting cage, don't just run to please your manager or your coach. Run with a purpose as you would in a game, remembering such fundamentals as hitting the inside part of the bag with your left foot as you cross over. When you throw the ball, play a game trying to hit your teammate in the chest. While you are warming up you can perfect your accuracy. If you are sloppy and wild in practice you might be the same way in the game, so don't goof off—make every throw count.

The same lessons apply in batting practice. Don't swing aimlessly at any pitch. If you hit the ball well, try to think what you did that was right. You probably met the ball out in front of the plate, kept your weight back and your head in, and took a level swing. If you hit the ball wrong, try to find out why. And whatever you do, don't overlook the art of bunting. If you don't think it's important, just wait until you get into a situation where you have to bunt to advance a runner. You'll find out in a hurry that this skill still belongs in baseball. The ability to bunt can become one of the most useful techniques you'll ever use. I've seen many games won by bunting, and I've suffered when others were lost because a player wasn't able to come through with a bunt.

What can a baseball-minded father do to develop his son into a Little League player? The first thing to do is to expose him to the game. If the interest isn't there, it's difficult to force it. Let him play with other boys in his neighborhood. In many cases it won't take much persuasion. One of the problems some parents face is to get their boys interested in other activities besides baseball. By contrast, I don't think there is anything worse than making a boy play baseball if he doesn't have the desire to do so. It's like forcing a boy to become a musician when his interests and talents lean toward an art career.

You can play catch with your boy at an early age. He'll enjoy the companionship and interest you show in him. It will help develop his reflexes and his coordination in throwing and fielding. You can use a tennis ball or a regulation-size sponge-rubber baseball and a lightweight bat. In this way he'll get the feel of playing without the fear of being hit by a hard ball.

Don't be alarmed if your boy is afraid of the ball. It's a natural tendency to shy away from ground balls and to step in the bucket at the plate. He'll overcome this with practice and maturity. Most professional players accept getting hit with the ball as part of the game, an occupational hazard. If we were afraid we wouldn't be in the majors.

Once your boy decides he wants to be a Little Leaguer, be sure to buy him a decent glove. He can't be expected to catch and field adequately with a flimsy $1.98 model. I don't know what you'll have to pay for a glove; your manager can help you with this selection. The point I'm making is that a boy needs a good glove—one that is large enough and will give him confidence in fielding grounders and catching fly balls. He'll probably keep it for two or three years, so it's a good initial investment. It will pay dividends for many months to come during his Little League career.

A favorable facet of Little League baseball is that the equipment and playing field are scaled to size. Even the circumference of the ball is a fraction less than a regulation major-league baseball. The infield dimensions are half those in the big leagues, the bases being 45 feet apart. In this way, young boys don't have impossible throws to make across the diamond, thus avoiding arm injuries.

If your boy wants to be a pitcher, let him. He'll need direction, however, and proper coaching. It's important for him to know how to hold the ball, how to push off from the rubber, how to follow through. There's quite a commotion among medical authorities over "Little League elbow," and this ailment should not be ignored. This condition is caused by boys throwing curves before their arms are mature enough to stand such a strain. Unless a boy is well developed, it is better for him to concentrate on control and straight, fast balls. Some parents refuse to let their boys pitch. In some cases this is probably a wise decision. An example on our own ball club is big Don Drysdale. When Don was a boy his dad kept him in the infield until he got into high school. When he switched to pitching he had a natural sweeping side-arm delivery which he attributes to his semiside-arm throws from second base to first.

Other injuries such as broken arms and legs have occurred in Little League. More serious accidents have resulted from players being hit by pitched or batted balls. With over 5 million boys participating in the program, the percentage of injuries has been comparatively low. These same accidents can and do happen on school playgrounds and sandlots so you can't put the finger on Little League exclusively as the cause of all boyhood injuries. Personally I'd rather have my boys playing Little League baseball with protective helmets and proper supervision than to have them hitching rides on the backs of trucks with their bicycles, playing in the street, or engaging in rock fights.

As a final word of advice to parents, especially fathers:

Don't expect too much from your boy, particularly if he's 10 years old or younger. Few, if any, boys are able to catch, field, throw, run, and hit with any appreciable skill until they are 11, 12, or older. Most boys at this age need more encouragement than anything else you can give them. And, managers, don't ever forget what Fred Haney said: "Let the boys have fun."

chapter · 12

Speaking of Spokane . . .

DURING MY YEARS in baseball, I've discovered another home besides home plate. As much as I like Los Angeles and living with Mr. Charles, ball players don't last forever, so in looking to the future when the Dodgers find a replacement for me, I have established a permanent residence in Spokane, Wash.

You can go so far in baseball—even reach great heights— but sooner or later you come to the point when the ball club starts looking around for someone to take your place. No matter how valuable you or any other player may be, there's always another waiting in the wings to replace you.

There's no assurance you'll stay with one ball club throughout your major-league career. A few players have been able to accomplish this, but the majority have not. When a player nears the end of his active career with one or two good seasons left, the front office is apt to trade him for a younger man who will develop and help the club for the next seven or eight years. A player can be on one team one day, be traded, and play against his former teammates the following day. It happens frequently.

I think a ball player is happier when he has one special town

97

or city he can call home. If he has children they also will
benefit from a feeling of security. That's one reason my wife
and I selected Spokane. My first trip to Spokane was in 1957
when I faced the Indians as a member of the Seattle Rainiers.
Being an outdoor enthusiast, it was love at first sight. This
beautiful pine-tree country is made for hunting and fishing,
my two favorite hobbies.

Spokane also proved to be my springboard to the Dodgers in
'59. On this 1959 team were such players as Ron Fairly, Don
Demeter, Frank Howard, Chuck Essegian, Roger Craig, and
Larry Sherry. Sherry's rise to fame as a major-leaguer should
inspire every minor-league player. At Spokane his 1958 record
was a dismal six wins and 14 losses. A year later he was in the
big leagues and the pitching star of the World Series with an
earned run average of 0.71 against the White Sox. It only
proves that if a player has the courage and the desire to
improve himself, he can go right to the top.

Larry didn't sit home and stew over his poor season of '58.
Instead, he came back strong the following spring with a
slider which was to become his big pitch. Although a trifle
wild, he also had a good fast ball. He had to take something
off of it, however, to get it over the plate. So he worked on his
control and developed the slider which was a new pitch for
him. There was no stopping him after that as he sparked our
pennant drive and established himself as one of the better
pitchers in the game.

Roger Craig showed the baseball world how important it
was for a player to develop the proper attitude. In 1959 he
was farmed out to Spokane after several years on the Dodgers.
Some players might have become discouraged and tossed in
the towel, but not Craig. He worked on specific techniques to
improve his pitching, and when he came back to the Dodgers
he won several key games. He contributed a great deal to our
successful championship bid at the end of the season.

Ron Fairly and Frank Howard are two other Dodgers whom
I admire for their spirit and hustle. Ron was with the Dodgers

in '59, but in 1960 he was sent back to Spokane. He didn't resent being demoted. Instead he took advantage of the opportunity to play every day and picked up the necessary experience he was lacking. By playing regularly he improved in all departments, had a great year, and is now one of the better players in the National League.

Howard is in a class by himself. He's got all the physical requirements: a great arm, good running speed, and as much power as anyone living or dead. He's also one of the most determined men I've ever known. Included among his accomplishments is a 562-foot home run at Pittsburgh. Frank has a tendency to underestimate his own ability. He is shy and modest. This is a pleasant contrast to some players whose names escape me but who never stop reminding you how "great" they are. Most of us on the Dodgers feel that Frank is a year or two away from greatness. Once he realizes he's one of the better players in the majors he'll relax a little, stop pressing, and go on to even greater achievements. We call Howard, Mr. Clean, after the giant on the liquid-detergent bottle. Opposing pitchers have other names for him.

Another Spokane teammate in 1959 was Chuck Essegian who is now showing the American League his power as a member of the Cleveland Indians. Chuck, a former Stanford All-America football star, is a natural athlete. He's such a good hitter, he should play every day. The Indians found that out. When he was with the Dodgers, his fielding was criticized. He didn't let that bother him. Instead, he kept in shape and when we needed him he came through like a real pro. His feat of hitting two pinch home runs against the White Sox set a World Series record. After his big year in '62 with Cleveland it looks like he'll be around for awhile.

With all of these ex-Spokane Indians in the majors it's not uncommon to return home each fall to find the townspeople hashing over the recent baseball campaigns in the middle of football season. They watch the Dodgers occasionally on the TV *Game of the Week* and follow every Dodger game via radio with Vin Scully and Jerry Doggett. Although Spokane is more than 1,000 miles from Los Angeles there's a certain type of radio that picks up Dodger station KFI, and many fans in Spokane have purchased this special unit. My wife and children listen to every Dodger game.

One of my off-season activities in Spokane is working with the local ball club in a public-relations capacity. Spencer Harris, the general manager, and Nave Lein, the business manager of the Spokane club, are two wonderful men who have done a lot to promote the Dodger farm team in the Northwest. We visit all the service clubs in the city during the winter months talking baseball and showing films of the 1959 World Series. (This is a film I really enjoy because I always know who's going to win!) Nave has helped me with my public speaking, something I had to learn from necessity. It's a wonderful thing to be able to speak in front of an audience, and I appreciate the help and confidence he's given me in mastering this art.

My favorite sport in Spokane is hunting. I have an arsenal of 11 guns and a German shorthair hunting dog named Ike. Spokane is the bustling hub of a 200-mile area known as the Inland Empire, a hunter's paradise. With lakes, streams, tall timber, and mountains, you can take your choice of hunting mule deer or elk, or, if you prefer, you can go after ducks and geese. Erwin Brockman of Brock's Suburban Agency and Bob Maker, sports editor of the *Cour de Lane Press,* are two of my best hunting and fishing friends. I've never seen Brockman miss a shot in five years, and if we ever get invaded, I'm glad he's on our side. He helped me and my family settle in the Valley of Spokane where we have a comfortable family home. (We have five children, and I can't think of a better place to raise them.) Maker follows my progress with the Dodgers, and converts my activities on a local plane with excellent coverage in his sports section.

Being a baseball player and in the public eye has some disadvantages as well as advantages, but I've always felt the benefits outweigh the drawbacks by far. One advantage I've found is that I've never run out of friends in Spokane who want to take me hunting. Most of the residents have farms, ranches, and land back in the hills where they have become intimately acquainted with the habits of various wild animals. They know where the deer stay, where they feed. They know the best lakes for fishing, where they are biting, and the type of bait or lures to use.

A friend may phone to tell me he knows where the deer are and to be at his home by six the next morning. I'm at the prescribed place on time as requested and a big herd of mule deer will pass in front of us on schedule at 6:35 A.M. To me this beats getting out and beating the brush. It's also a lot safer because the men I hunt with are experts and know exactly at what they're shooting. These friends have been wonderful to me and my family.

One of my bird-hunting friends, Vance Hurt, lives down by Union Flats, a short distance from Spokane. His home is on a farm in the middle of a big wheat field where the great Canadian geese come in to feed. We'll hike about 150 yards, crawl into some pits he has dug, and within 15 minutes the skies are black with hundreds of geese. The other way to hunt geese is to spot them, dig your pits, or, if there is snow on the ground, hide under a sheet and hope they'll make an appearance. Vance always spots them when they come on his property, so rather than rough it in a cold tent, we sleep in a warm, comfortable home and go out early and bag our limit.

I also enjoy playing golf, but found that my golfing partners aren't as nice to me as my hunting and fishing friends because I haven't run across any of them yet who are willing to give me any strokes.

The Spokane Chamber of Commerce honored me as its top citizen at the end of the 1962 season. I suspect my neighbor, Vic Felice, an attorney, had a hand in this. It was a pleasant surprise to return home after such a grueling summer and find the townspeople receiving me in such a gracious manner. As a contrast, I remember in 1959 how the citizens of San Francisco were ready to dump me off the Golden Gate Bridge for the big series I had against the Giants.

Spokane is known as the Friendly City, and it is well named. The school system is excellent. The bus picks up my children in front of the house and drops them off after school. My oldest boy plays football, basketball, and baseball. He was playing baseball one day at school and made an error. His coach told him his dad was a major-league ball player, and that he should be able to catch the ball better than he had shown. This apparently happened a few times. Finally, my son stopped and told the coach, with all due respect, that his name was Barry Wills, not Maury Wills.

My younger boy also broke up the class when they were filling out special forms at the beginning of the semester. The teacher asked Elliot what kind of work his daddy did, to which he replied: "My daddy doesn't work, he plays ball!"

chapter • 13

Brains and Brass

WALT ALSTON CAN manage any team of mine any place, any time. I only hope I'm there to play for him. During my short stay with the Dodgers I have thoroughly enjoyed our association. You'll find people who will question his ability as a manager, but this is to be expected. He can't field for us, or pitch, or throw, or bat for us; all he can do is give us direction. Back through history, baseball or otherwise, leaders have been criticized. Our national pastime isn't always baseball; it's often known as second-guessing. If thousands of people can question the President of the United States, then baseball managers, including Walt Alston, shouldn't become too alarmed over a few stray verbal darts tossed in their direction.

I've mentally questioned some of Walt's decisions, but I've refused to jump to conclusions. With only a few years in the majors I don't feel qualified to judge the ability of a man who has been managing a big-league team for a decade. He has been the most successful of all Dodger managers, a point in his favor. Since I've been with the Dodgers he's treated me as well, if not better, than I ever would have expected.

103

When I first came up to the Dodgers in '59, I was in and out of the line-up, alternating with Don Zimmer and becoming more than a little despondent. I finally went to Alston one day and requested a transfer back to Spokane where I could play every day and be home with my family. It wasn't fun, even though I was wearing a Dodger uniform, to sit on the bench and not know whether I would become a regular.

"I don't seem to be helping the club too much. Do you think it would be better for me to be playing regularly at Spokane?" I asked him.

"Keep your chin up. Let's see how things develop. You've shown me a lot. I have to keep juggling the line-up to put my best men in spots where I think they can help us the most. Don't get discouraged," he said.

Several times since then—after I had become a full-fledged major-leaguer, Walt reminded me of this incident and how happy he was that I decided to take his advice and remain in the majors. Of course, I thanked him because I don't think it would have taken too much persuasion at the time to get him to ship me back to Spokane. I just wasn't that brilliant a ball player. He must have seen something in me that I had overlooked. I've since learned it not only pays to steal, it also pays to look in the mirror once in awhile.

I know that as far as handling men, no one is better at it than Walt Alston. He doesn't crack a whip or needle us. He treats us like men, and expects us to act that way. Sometimes we act like boys, but at least he gives us credit for being mature. He doesn't watch over us, and few Dodgers ever have taken advantage of him.

It's easy for ball players to pop off that another manager might be more suitable for our team. I can't go along with that, however, because Alston's record alone defies comparison. People in different capacities have different personalities. One man might make a great coach but would be a poor manager. Another might be a good field manager but would be unsuitable as a general manager. Some men make great scouts but would be completely lost directing play from the dugout. It's almost like judging ball players. You get a different perspective of a player when he's playing against you. You only see him some times during the season. This means there are 144 games when you don't see him. It's pretty hard to make an honest evaluation under these conditions. You can get a pretty good indication of a man's abilities in these few games, but it would be false judgment to predicate everything on such limited viewing. When you play alongside someone for 162 games you get the correct picture of this man. It's the same way with your manager. The fan in the stands can voice his opinion, but he's not qualified to judge because he really doesn't know what circumstances are involved.

When I'm asked how I like certain managers it's difficult to give an honest answer unless I've played for them. Unless you've performed for them, lived with them, and suffered with them, it's almost impossible to analyze their managerial ability accurately.

One of my favorites is Mrs. Walt Alston. She has been a wonderful friend to my wife and often sits with her at Dodger Stadium.

Walt Alston is also a gracious host. We were off one day in Cincinnati in 1961, and had nothing planned, so Walt invited the team to his ranch in Darrtown. He chartered a special bus for the 40-minute ride from downtown Cinci, and we had a blast. We rode his horses, ate like his pigs, and thoroughly enjoyed ourselves. Walt took us down to his gun club where we did some trap shooting. I learned then that not only could he manage a ball club but he could also handle a shotgun. He's a tremendous shot. He broke 25 clay pigeons in as many attempts, which is batting 1.000 in my league. It was my baptism as a trap shooter, and I popped 20 out of 25 plus 14 doubles. When you start shooting doubles and hitting them consistently you're in another class because they are difficult to hit. We topped off this memorable outing with a big family-style dinner at the local church.

During spring training Walt permits a lot of the players to get in shape on their own. Some players require more time than others and have their own routines. He has enough confidence in them to know they'll be ready in time for opening day.

Several times during the 1962 season he stopped me on my way to lead off to find out if I thought I could steal on the pitcher. If I told him I could, he would tell me to go ahead rather than have Jim Gilliam sacrifice me to second. Once on second, Jim could bunt me to third. Then I could score on a long fly ball, a hit, or an infield out. The fact that he relied on my judgment inspired me with confidence. The thing that pleased me the most, however, was that I was able to come through for him almost every time. You'd think we planned it that way. As long as he was going to rely on my opinion the least I could do was to make him look good. His faith in my ability to steal was evidenced in my record-breaking game against the Cardinals. It was my last chance, and even though I was injured and we were behind, I don't think I ever ran harder or faster in my whole life. It really made me feel great to know that he was pulling for me.

Walt also was considerate of my general health and well-being on several occasions during the rugged '62 campaign. I remember in cities like Houston and St. Louis, which can feel like the inside of a pressure cooker in July or August, Alston let me sleep an hour later and take a cab to the park. He knew I wasn't as physically strong as some of the other players and that the strain of playing in every game was wearing me down. When I did report to the club, I loosened up a bit and was ready to start the ball game. Many times he let me skip infield practice, which was another big concession on his part because when you get to know Walt Alston you know he isn't the type of manager who likes to see any of his players loung-

ing around. I feel the same way. It's better to keep active.
It looks better, and it keeps a ball club alert.

We see quite a lot of Dodger owner Walter O'Malley during
spring training. While he doesn't put on a uniform and work
out with the ball club, he participates in all other activities
including meals and evening movies. He stands in the chow
line like everyone else even though it might take 30 minutes
for him to be served. When he and Mrs. O'Malley attend
the movies he gets in line in front of the auditorium along with
the rest of us. If there's a seat available for him he sits down;
if not he has to stand.

He's been most generous with our food tab. When teams are
traveling the league calls for a $10-per-day, per-player meal
allowance. Many of the clubs issue their players a flat $10.
The Dodgers permit us to sign tabs, which means we can
exceed the $10 limit if the check is greater than this total.
More often than not we go over. In some cities, dinner alone
can come close to this amount.

I formed another favorable opinion of Mr. O'Malley during
the 1959 World Series. As soon as we won the play-off game
from Milwaukee, he chartered a special plane just for the
players' wives and flew them back to Chicago for the first two
games of the series. They also had hotel reservations waiting
for them. None of us was billed for this expense. This is in
contrast to one of the eastern teams whose players discovered
there was a deduction for transportation and hotel accommodations when they received their World Series checks. Mr.
O'Malley was all set to treat the wives again in '62, but the
boys from Frisco had other plans.

Successful men like to surround themselves with competent
assistants. Such is the case with the Dodgers and the general
manager, E. J. (Buzzie) Bavasi. I've always admired him.
There's no end to what this man has done for me. He was the
one who made the decision to bring me to the Dodgers from
Spokane when Don Zimmer and Bobby Lillis weren't going too
well, and he felt the club needed help at short. Two months

later he still was looking for a shortstop when fortunately I came through for him. He gave me every possible opportunity to prove that I was a big leaguer, and I'm glad now that I could live up to his earlier expectations.

One of the most humiliating things that can happen to a ball player is for him to pick up a paper and learn that he's being sent back to the minors, or, worse yet, given his unconditional release. Sooner or later you expect these things to happen. But when they do, you like to hear about it firsthand from the front office and not from a reporter or a fan on the street. I know for sure that there's never been a Dodger who ever found out from other sources so long as Buzzie Bavasi was general manager. He's the first one to contact the ball player. Not only will Buzzie tell him, but he'll also discuss it. He explains the ball club's position and why this particular trade or move was made. I've yet to hear an ex-Dodger ever say anything derogatory about Bavasi. Everyone I've spoken with, including Gil Hodges, Roger Craig, Norm Larker, and Don Zimmer, have remarked that he's one of the finest men they've ever dealt with in baseball. I feel exactly the same way.

When I went into his office to sign my 1963 contract, I knew I was going to receive a substantial increase over my '62 salary. I was full of confidence, but by the time I departed he had me feeling that I was lucky to be wearing a Dodger uniform. I didn't feel badly about it, because I got a nice raise—it's just that he is one of the most persuasive men I've ever met. He's just great. I've yet to sign a contract for what I requested, yet when I did I was pleased and satisfied with the figure at which we arrived at. This is as it should be because, as I've mentioned, a player can't be at his best if he isn't content.

Unfortunately, every time Buzzie joins us on the road I seem to have a bad day. It's ironical the way this happens. Normally I play better away from home. I almost hate to hear he's in a city where we're playing because I probably can count on a poor performance.

You can't be with the Dodgers five minutes without learning

something new about baseball from Leo Durocher. He's helped me a lot—not with special instruction or coaching but merely by being around him. You have only to listen to him to detect his enormous desire to win, to outsmart the other ball players and the other ball club. In my opinion, he's one of the most intelligent baseball men that ever lived. When you hear him talk you learn how he makes the other manager commit himself first, how he thinks four or five innings ahead while he's making changes on the field. He reminds me of a good card player making an early move that pays off later in the game. Leo makes you aware of how important this strategy can be. He makes you think. Suddenly you realize there's more to baseball than hitting, running, fielding, and throwing. Leo just won't tolerate mental mistakes. He realizes that a player will make errors, will miss the ball, or throw wild, or strike out. These he accepts without question, but to goof by throwing to the wrong base or loafing or missing signs or fouling up key plays, then he really blows up. He lets you know about it, too. One thing about Leo: you know immediately where you stand with him.

Durocher and other coaches on our club have the authority to act at any time. If he feels you deserve to be told off, he's just the man who can do it. I think this is the way it should be. A ball player can go along for months thinking he's doing the right thing, and unless some one tells him otherwise he might be completely wrong. Leo is important to our ball club in this respect because we have a lot of young ball players, and most of them are learning. I know I'm still taking instruction and want to continue to do so. I dread the day when I stop learning, because that's the time when I better hang up the spikes.

One of the important assignments of Joe Becker, our pitching coach, is to keep the pitchers in top physical condition. Pitching can take a lot out of you, and even today with all the relief help available a pitcher needs plenty of strength and stamina. Joe runs the pitchers in the outfield, and I join

them at least three days a week. This might seem unusual—
that I exert myself when I need as much rest as possible—
but it's also important for me to loosen my leg muscles before
a ball game. Every three or four days, my legs will tighten
up. So I have to run until they limber up again. It's a
cycle I go through all season long. Joe hits fungoes, keeps
track of the pitching rotation, and makes the bull pen assignments. He also hits me a few flies each day.

Greg Mulleavy, our first base coach, is one of the finest
instructors of infield play in the game. I've known Greg from
my minor-league days when he first put me through the
grinder in spring training at Vero Beach. Greg is a real
pro, and I've always been able to learn a lot from him. During
infield practice when I'm fielding balls from Pete Reiser, Greg
will stand five or ten feet away from me watching every move
I make while at the same time feeding balls to the batting
practice pitcher. He'll holler to me telling me the mistakes
I'm making. Sometimes I'll go to him for advice when I feel
I'm doing something wrong, and he straightens me out. Perhaps I'm crossing over too fast, or I might not be staying down
on the ball long enough, or maybe my feet are too close
together, or my hands are in the wrong position—whatever
it is, he can detect it and doesn't hesitate to tell me. I respect
his judgment and am glad to have him show this kind of
interest in me, as well as in the entire ball club. There are
hundreds of things you can do wrong without even trying.
It's good to eliminate these bad fielding habits before they
affect your over-all play.

We kid Greg a lot about his job—keeping track of the
baseballs. This is a big item and one of the greatest single
expenses a club faces each season. Each ball costs more than
$2, and when one goes in the stands, it's lost. The Dodgers
use some $30,000 worth of baseballs each year, enough to pay
salaries for two or three players. Mulleavy takes his assignment seriously. We hide them on him and rib him often,
but we know it's an important job.

While I was home in the fall of 1962 recovering from the shock of the Dodgers missing their second World Series in four years, I received the good news that Bobby Bragan had been named to manage the Milwaukee Braves. I wrote to him immediately to tell him how pleased I was and to wish him well. In my book, Bragan is a natural leader. It must have been difficult for him to serve as a coach, because where ball players are involved he's at his best when he's top man. The Braves have the potential to be one of the better clubs in the National League. They have some fine young pitching talent to go along with the power hitting of Eddie Mathews and Hank Aaron. If Bobby can get the Braves to play as well as most observers think they can, Milwaukee is bound to come up with a winner.

A lot will depend upon how fast he can bring his kid pitchers along. If I were a manager this would be one of my toughest assignments—handling pitchers. The other eight men know how to play the game. They know how to react under all circumstances—when to play for the bunt, the double play and other key defensive moves, but pitching is a different story. I think Bragan will do a good job in this department. He seems to know when to leave the pitcher in and when to bring a fresh one from the bull pen. He's also an inspiring type of manager who gives his pitchers the confidence they need to win. He'll make them all feel like Warren Spahn on his best day. He'll make them believe in themselves. That's what he did for me when I was in the minors. If he hadn't given me this rejuvenation I wouldn't be in the majors. Bragan restored my confidence and my faith, and every time we play the Braves I'll try to make him regret it.

It will feel strange to play against Bobby, the man who picked me up when I was down. He's always wished me the best personally, and I've always reciprocated.

He knows a lot of my base-stealing secrets; after all, he taught me some of them. He also knows my hitting strengths and weaknesses, but he's not alone in this respect. You can't stay in the league too long before every pitcher has his own book on you. A pitcher may not be able to get the ball where he wants it every time, but he knows where and how he should pitch to you and every other batter.

I know the type of ball Bragan plays, so we break even in outguessing each other. Bobby likes to play a running game: the hit and run and stealing. We never let sentiment interfere with our play, and neither of us would have much respect for the other if we didn't go all out to win. This is what he taught me. I know he would be upset if I didn't follow this advice to the letter.

When Jackie Robinson came to the Dodgers there was considerable opposition, not only from the other ball clubs but on the Brooklyn team as well. One of the players mentioned prominently in this conspiracy was Bobby Bragan, then a catcher for the Dodgers. I found this so hard to believe that I approached Bobby one day to ask him if it were true.

"They tell me you were one of the ringleaders in a group on the Dodgers opposed to Jackie Robinson; is this true?" I asked him.

"Maury, all I can say is that I was on the Dodgers at the time. I was friendly with the group that tried to keep Robinson in the minors, so, naturally I was implicated. There were some troublemakers to be sure, but I wasn't one of them."

Bobby is as close to me as my own brother. He sends me a Christmas card each year addressed "To My Boy Maury," and there's nothing I wouldn't do for him regardless of the request. His word on Robinson was good enough for me. I can't believe he would deliberately go out of his way to hurt anyone. He's too fine a man. He's also a man who thinks for himself. I was glad he straightened me out on this matter because it was something that had bothered me considerably.

It's good to have Charlie Dressen back with the Dodgers again. He helped me a lot when I joined the club in 1959. He had Pee Wee Reese help me on the technique of feeding the ball to the second baseman on the double play. Dressen also showed me how to improve the cut-off play from the field. His instruction paid off handsomely in the '59 World Series with Chicago. In fact, Casey Stengel and many other baseball experts said the play I made against Sherm Lollar was the turning point in the series.

As you may recall, the Sox had swamped us in the opener, 11-0, and were threatening again in the middle of the second game. Lollar was on first and started circling the bases on a double hit past Wally Moon in left field. Just as Moon fielded the ball, I took a split-second glance over my shoulder and noticed that the coach was waving Lollar home. As soon as I took the relay throw from Wally, I knew exactly what to do. I spun and fired home to John Roseboro who had Lollar trapped by some 15 or 20 feet. It was one of the clutch plays in that game, as well as in the entire series, which we won rather handily after that shaky start.

Under most circumstances you can depend on another in-fielder to yell and tell you where the ball should be thrown off the relay. However, when 50,000 fans are screaming, you can't hear above the roar so you have to look and decide yourself where you'll go with the ball before it arrives from the outfield. This was one of the inside tips that Charlie Dressen taught me, and it was a valuable one. This is smart baseball, the kind for which Dressen is noted.

Dressen also helped me a lot with my attitude. I was a little too relaxed, too casual when I first joined the Dodgers. He warned me that this was the big time and that I'd better get on the ball and go all out to win. He told me to be sharp and emphasized how important it was to win. He also kept our spirits up when we'd lose a few and reminded us of some of the darker days in the past when things were really rough. He told us how others snapped their slumps by relaxing at a movie or with some other light diversion. He helped us forget our worries, and before we knew it we were back again playing like champions.

Two nonplaying members of our ball club are Vin Scully

and Jerry Doggett, two real pros in the radio-television sports-casting field. These men have been most generous in their praise of me, so much so that several fans have embarrassed me by asking if they were on my payroll. Both Vin and Jerry travel with us from the beginning of the spring-training exhibition season until the end of the regular schedule. Most of my contact with them has been in pregame or postgame interviews. One of the few times I've caught their broadcast was back in 1960 when I was taken out of the game in the early innings. I knew then for the first time why so many fans take their transistors to the ball game—to double their pleasure. I don't think you'll find a better baseball announcer anywhere than Vin Scully, and the millions of fans in Los Angeles seem to feel the same way. He's a great one.

I get a lot of personal satisfaction when I can do something noteworthy which Vin and Jerry can pass on to the fans in the hospitals, or in convalescent rest homes, men in veterans hospitals, the crippled or the blind, those who can't get out to the games. These Dodger boosters have to rely on these two experts to give them a graphic description of the action. So any time I can make a good fielding play, or steal a base, or get a key hit, I'm thrilled to know that we're all doing something to make a lot of other people happy. That's incentive enough for me to try to turn in a peak performance.

chapter • 14

Road Trip

On D-Day (Departure Day) minus seven—Lee Scott, the Dodgers' traveling secretary, brings around the itineraries and passes them out to the players. I give this some thought considering the number of cities we'll visit and the number of days we'll be there. I try to plan my wardrobe and figure what I'll need to complete the junket. Most of us take as little as possible and rely on the dry-cleaners to keep us looking neat. I also found out that if you take too much luggage it can be a burden to you in tracking it down each time you move into a new city.

Many times on our way east we stop at San Francisco, then work our way back toward the midwest, stopping at St. Louis, Chicago, Cincinnati, and Milwaukee. With the National League expanded to ten teams we saw a lot of the U.S.A. last season. Because the schedule was drawn up at the last minute, it was impossible to follow any set pattern and we found ourselves jumping around on an irregular basis. For example, we might be in the midwest, then in Philadelphia, and from there head straight home.

In flying our own plane we didn't have to depend upon

the various airline departure schedules. As a group we decided whether we would remain in the same town or fly to the next city. A lot would depend on the distance we had to travel and the schedule facing us. We might be off for an entire 24 hours, which would give us the equivalent of a day off. Oftentimes we'd pull into a city at 2 or 3 A.M., and before we settled down the bell captain was at the door with our luggage, so we were about ready for sleep when the sun came up. Before we complain too loudly we're reminded that this still beats the all-night bus trips that many ball clubs endure in the lower classifications. I'd like to forget a few of them myself—they were really rugged.

The run from Chicago to Milwaukee is a pleasant one. All games at Chicago's Wrigley Field are during the day (no lights). Thus we either can fly up to Beer Town or take a bus or a train. We usually play night games, so we have considerable free time to rest or visit friends or relatives.

Once we arrive at our hotel there's a mad scramble at the newsstand for the stack of 20 or 25 papers. Then one of us checks the mail while another gets the room keys. John Roseboro was my roommate last year. The sportswriters have nicknamed him Gabby. I get a yes or a no out of him now and then. John and I usually eat most of our meals in our hotel room. By taking advantage of room service we can get a good long rest. Once in a while we'll take in a movie or I'll visit one of the local music shops to pick up some sheet music for my banjo.

During the 1962 season I didn't have much opportunity to pursue my music because there usually were reporters tracking me down for a story. They wanted to know if I thought I could break the record; if so, the actual number I would steal. This was almost impossible to answer. Most of them wanted to know the toughest pitchers to steal against. I didn't mind giving them this information, but I was hesitant to name those who were the easiest.

Newspapermen are an important phase of baseball. It's

a game that can be interpreted many different ways. Even though fans turn out by the thousands they still enjoy reading the sidelights and highlights of each game whether or not they attend in person. I found the reporters on the road very friendly. I tried to be coöperative and help them with their assignments. The Dodgers have traditionally been good copy, and I know our '62 club with Frank Howard, Tommy and Willie Davis, Don Drysdale, and Sandy Koufax all creating interest with their play, plus my own exploits, helped carry on this tradition. The big attendance mark which we posted is strong evidence of this competitive excitement.

Selfishly, I was disappointed not to be able to pursue my music career. Early in the season I carried my guitar and a ukelele and was able to practice in my free time. Once it appeared I was headed toward a record, my time ceased to be my own. In fact, after the first all-star game in Washington, D.C., I left the instruments home.

One of the diversions I had while on the road, if you could call it that, was to answer my fan mail. My wife and I answered every piece of mail during the season. Ironically, Sid Ziff mentioned this in his column in the Los Angeles Times one day, and almost overnight our mail count was doubled. We figure we averaged 2,000 letters a month. I used to write home every day to Gert, but the pressure became so intense that I had to cut down to four or five times a week. We also get a lot of mail while we are on the road. The fans find out where the Dodgers are staying, and most of us find a stack of mail waiting in each city. I bought picture post cards to answer most of my mail. In this way it didn't pile up, and I didn't have to bring so much home with me. My wife played a big part in this assignment, and if it hadn't been for her I don't think it would have gotten answered. Running a home, taking care of five children, and keeping track of my correspondence kept her busy.

We travel by bus from the hotel to the airport unless we get special permission to take a cab. The bus leaves at 5 P.M.

sharp for the night games and 11 A.M. for the day games.
When they say sharp, they mean it. The bus waits for no one,
not even Mr. O'Malley. If anyone is late his best bet would be
to cab it out to the stadium.

We have the same strict time schedules in flying from the
various airports. I remember a hysterical incident in 1959
when Don Zimmer was late arriving at Cincinnati Airport.
He was running full speed trying to climb aboard while our
plane was taxiing down the runway. The pilot refused to stop
for him, so Zip had to get to the next city at his own expense.

This is the way the Dodgers operate—and I'm in favor of
it. It's a good policy because it's fair to everyone. We have
our laughs—especially when one of the players knows his
roommate is on the way down from the hotel room—but
more often than not the bus will pull out and leave one or two
players standing at the curb. Even if the bus driver wants to
wait, the other players will holler for him to take off, especially if some of them have been the victims of previous tardi-
ness. Once in a while a player will slip through at the last
second and thus earn a big round of applause.

Each time we open a series on the road, we have clean
uniforms waiting for us, our shoes are shined, and our equipment is waiting for us in the visiting clubhouse by the time we
arrive. John Griffin works with the other clubhouse attendant,
and between the two of them they take care of both clubs.
As soon as we're dressed, we assemble for a meeting. We go
over the hitters, and discuss the pitcher and other facets about
the opposing ball club. We might confer once more in this
same city if manager Alston thinks it is necessary.

We have quite a contingent with us on each road trip. In
addition to the playing personnel, the managerial staff, the
trainers, our official Dodger statistician—Allen Roth, Frank
Finch of the Los Angeles *Times,* Bob Hunter of the Los Angeles
Herald-Examiner, George Lederer of the Long Beach *Inde-
pendent-Press-Telegram,* and our two sportscasters, Vin Scully
and Jerry Doggett, there'll be 15 or 20 other passengers. Our

plane seats many passengers and is usually filled to capacity
with relatives of the ball players, friends of Mr. O'Malley or
Buzzie Bavasi, and other dignitaries.

A Dodger tradition (or superstition) is that each player has
the same seat on each trip. I'll never forget the first time I
boarded the plane back in '59 when I took Duke Snider's seat.
Duke and Gil Hodges had been flying together for some five
or six years. So as I climbed aboard I slid in beside Gil and
started talking with him. A few minutes later Duke came by
and asked if he might have his seat. Not knowing they were
assigned, I was hesitant in getting up. So he told me to forget
it, and moved toward the back. When Gil Hodges explained
to me that the seats were assigned I wanted to crawl into the
baggage compartment. I got up immediately, apologized to
Duke, and insisted that he return to his seat. He said to skip
it. I've never forgotten my embarrassment, but the same thing
has since happened to me.

Before the Dodgers purchased the present plane, an Electra
jet, we used to charter a DC6B, and Charley Neal and I always
sat together on this plane. One day I climbed aboard and
found Mr. and Mrs. O'Malley sitting in our places with
Charley up front a couple of rows. I gave Charley a quizzical
look as if to say, "What's going on here?"

"You tell them to get out of our seats," he said. "Oh, no,
I'm not going to do that," I responded.

Not to be outdone, and in a voice that could be heard by
the entire ball club, Charley boomed: "Mr. O'Malley, Maury
said you got his seat."

About this time I slid into the back of the plane and became
an integral part of the fuselage.

Our present plane has every modern comfort and convenience. We have hot meals, coffee, lemonade, soft drinks.
There's a lounge in the back of the plane and one up forward
where various groups play hearts and bridge. Wally Moon,
Duke Snider, Don Drysdale and a couple of others always
take over the front lounge. The younger players occupy the

rear lounge. Manager Alston and his coaches normally sit in the center section.

We not only fly first class but we have the best maintained Electra jet in the country. Every place we stop we get special maintenance service. The players seem to enjoy the plane trips. I hear few complaints, if any. Our plane has four sleeping berths; two lowers and two uppers. If a pitcher is scheduled to start the next day he might stretch out for an extra nap or rest. When big Frank Howard gets sleepy he takes up two bunks.

I often go into the pilot's compartment. I've spent so much time there that I honestly believe I could fly the plane if I had to. We have a great crew, and it's amazing to see the way they jockey the plane around to duck bad weather. When you're in the passengers' section you aren't a bit conscious of this, but sitting up forward I can see every move they make.

We have a ball every time we play the New York Mets. The team is loaded with ex-Dodgers and, of course, there's no one in baseball quite like Casey Stengel. Roger Craig is one of the first to greet me. He will inform me that he has a new move to stop me and pick me off first. When questioned about it, he said he'd hit me in the legs.

"Stay low, Maury. I'd hate to hit you in the head," advises Charley Neal when I first meet him. "I like to throw underhand to first, and I'm afraid you might get low-bridged."

When Joe Pignatano caught for the Mets in '62 he claimed he knew just how to pitch to me. As I recall that was on Memorial Day, the day I tied the National League record by hitting two home runs in the same game, each from a different side of the plate.

It's the same story when we play in Houston—more former Dodgers. While Norm Larker has been traded and Bobby Bragan has moved up to Milwaukee, it was a picnic for us when they were with the Colts. Bobby was a little reserved when he was with Houston because he didn't want to be accused by the Houston players of fraternizing with us. But he usually had a few comments for us before joining the home team in the dugout. Norm Larker was always the rugged individualist, yakking and griping. Same old Norm. But his bark usually was more vicious than his bite. He's really a good-natured guy. He's all heart. With Norm on first in front of the Dodger dugout he took a pretty good roasting from his old teammates.

Norm and I had a tiff going back in '59 when he accidentally hit me with a ground ball while I was taking infield practice. We exchanged a few words, but it never went any further than that. The "feud" got into the papers, and was blown way out of proportion.

During one of our '62 games at Houston, he cuffed me with the glove fairly hard on a pick-off play. When I questioned him about this, he stepped back off the bag to inform me that we weren't playing tiddelywinks—that this was base-ball and I'd better expect a few hard knocks. We swapped a few jibes, and continued with the game. You always can count on some kind of a commotion when Larker is involved.

My favorite out-of-town ball park is a tossup between Forbes Field, Pittsburgh, and Connie Mack Stadium, Philadelphia. The State of Pennsylvania has been good to me. I have managed to hit .400 or better in each of these cities each season. I like the lights in Philadelphia. The stands are close to the foul lines, and give me a compact feeling. I never have had any trouble following the ball there, and always seem to have a good series. Playing in Connie Mack Stadium also has given me an opportunity to perform in front of my family. They often charter a bus to come over from nearby Washington, D.C. As fate would have it, I've come up with some of my finest games with my relatives in attendance. I've had three or four hits in a game, stolen a base or two, and made good fielding plays. One of my biggest days was on a Sunday in August 1960. I collected seven hits in ten at bats, scored four runs, batted in two others, and stole four bases. We beat the Phillies twice, 8-7 and 2-1. Bobby Bragan later told me about a conversation he had with Al Barlick following this double-header.

"That was some show. I'd have to say Wills is the best infielder in baseball today," Barlick told him.

Forbes Field, home of the Pittsburgh Pirates, always has been home to me. I don't know what causes me to play well there. The lights aren't any better, and the field isn't superior to any other ball park. The playing surface is hard-packed, and I've managed to hit a lot of line drives through the infield. Bob Prince, radio voice of the Pirates, has been ribbing me about my hits. He calls me a banjo hitter, but I remind him that they all look alike in print. If anything, Bob has helped me because I've been treated well by the fans in this city. I think our friendly feud has worked to my advantage. Maybe if the Pirate management knew this they'd have the people give me the business. The fans in Pittsburgh are great. They've always shown good sportsmanship. As long as we couldn't win the flag in '60, I'm glad the Pirates came through. It was good for baseball, and the fact that they beat the Yankees made it a perfect ending to a great year for them.

My favorite city (I said city, not ball park) is San Francisco. There's something about the atmosphere that's different from any other large city in the country. In my opinion, it's the most beautiful city I've ever seen. The tall buildings, Chinatown, the high hills, the towering bridges, blue bay, the waterfront, the cable cars, yes, even the fog, make it a fascinating place to visit. There are a million things to see and do. It's always cool there, even in summer. You might get laughed at for taking a topcoat to San Francisco in August, but you'll be glad you did. I like cool weather; that's one reason I enjoy living in Spokane. San Francisco is very cosmopolitan, and it has some of the finest restaurants in the west.

One of my long-range ambitions is to fish for striped bass in San Francisco Bay. The thought of fishing throughout the

Bay area has really fascinated me. I'm going to plan a stop-over on one of my trips to or from Spokane.

The National League expansion program has worked wonderfully well for the ball players themselves. There are 50 more jobs available. It has enabled many more men from the minor leagues to move up, especially those with the AAA clubs who were capable of playing major-league ball once they had the opportunity. There's also going to be a greater demand for veterans as clubs realize many of them are going to be difficult to replace. The league is bound to get stronger each year.

One of the difficulties I faced in going for the stolen-base record was the various conditions of the base paths in each National League ball park. In Chicago, for example, the ground might be soft from a rain. I'd have to shuffle around watching the pitcher every second until I could find a firm foothold. I had no worries of this nature in Dodger Stadium; the ground was the same throughout the season. While one of the out-of-town infields might be poor for fielding, it was often excellent for sliding. If I became too discouraged over playing conditions I always could overcome this obstacle by thinking about Candlestick Park.

In the few short years I've been in the senior circuit, as it is affectionately referred to by the press, I've gathered increasing respect for many of my opponents. The following players have been selected by me personally as my all-opponent defensive team. This isn't necessarily the best team in the league, but the players listed are the ones that have given me the most trouble when I was at bat or running the bases:

Left Field: STAN MUSIAL, St. Louis. Musial plays me right along the left-field foul line. If I could pull the ball over short I'd have a triple every time, but I can't control my shots, and he's usually waiting to catch line drives right on the chalk mark. It's difficult to guide the ball, and in hitting away I seem to hit it to him nearly every time. Stan is also one of the all-time greats who makes you proud to be playing in a game with him.

Center Field: WILLIE MAYS, San Francisco. It's almost impossible to hit a pop-up in front of him or a fly ball in back of him. Only time I ever hit one over the center fielder's head against the Giants was when Mays was late coming to the park and Matty Alou was taking his place. Mays probably would have caught it in front of him. He has great reflexes, knowing exactly where the ball will land and when.

Right Field: FELIPE ALOU, San Francisco. He's made some great catches against me. I've hit some sharp line drives in Candlestick Park that would be triples elsewhere, but Alou has hauled them in. When I hit the long ball he seems to be playing me deep; if I hit line drives he's usually playing me shallow. He's a good one.

Third Base: KEN BOYER, St. Louis. I've laid down some excellent bunts (so I thought) against Boyer. He'd appear to be playing deep, but by the time the ball was hit he'd be right on top of it and would catch me at first more often than not. I've also hit some line drives down the third-base line that would normally go for triples, but he'd make impossible catches to rob me. I think I can cross him up by hitting away when he's in for the bunt, but he'll fade and snag a hot grounder.

Alternate Third Base: DON HOAK, Philadelphia. Don was so great playing against me when he was with Pittsburgh that I can't rightfully leave him off my defensive team. He's given me fits every time. He bobs back and forth from the pitcher to the base line trying to distract me. When I first look he'll be standing even with the pitcher, then as the pitcher winds up he's over by third. Someday I'll hit one off his shins.

Shortstop: JOSE PAGAN, San Francisco. This kid is about the most improved ball player in the league. The reason he's made so many good plays on me is because he's trying to take over as the top shortstop in the National loop. I admire him for this because this was what I went through when I was playing in the shadow of the sensational Ernie Banks. With Ernie now playing first base this was one way to take over the honor. Pagan also has hit well against us. The two often run together—hitting and fielding.

Second Base: BILL MAZEROSKI, Pittsburgh. At Pittsburgh they pitch me inside a lot, and when I pull the ball Maz is there ready to take it. He has a knack of being at the right place when the ball is hit. He's got a great pair of hands and always gets a good jump on the ball. I have a hard time hitting it past him.

First Base: BILL WHITE, St. Louis. This fellow is just uncanny the way he leaves his feet to spear line drives. He's at his best on drag bunts down the base line. In fact, I seldom try to bunt against the combination of White on first and Boyer at third. On top of this the Cards have some great fielding pitchers.

Catcher: CLAY DALRYMPLE, Philadelphia. This boy is sharp behind the plate. He has a strong, accurate arm. DICK BERTELL of the Chicago Cubs would be my alternate choice. He's been able to catch me stealing at times.

Pitchers: WARREN SPAHN, Milwaukee. A lot of people ask me how I do stealing against Spahn. This is hard to answer because I don't get on first often enough against him to give an honest answer. He's not only tough to steal on, he's primarily tough to hit against. JUAN MARICHAL, San Francisco. Quick moves to first, holds you on with constant throws (see chapter on Giants). ROGER CRAIG, New York. Has great moves to first. Picks a lot of base runners off each year. LARRY JACKSON, Chicago. Rough to hit against, equally difficult to steal off. One of my big thrills in breaking the N.L. stolen-base mark was that I had to steal two bases in my 156th game, and I was able to do just that against Jackson. BOBBY SHANTZ, Pittsburgh. Probably the best fielding pitcher in the league. Dynamite on bunts and slow rollers. Won Gold Glove Award as top fielder (pitcher) in '62.

chapter 15

L.A. Coliseum —
Dodger Stadium

I'LL NEVER FORGET the first time I walked onto the floor
of the Los Angeles Memorial Coliseum. I felt completely
insignificant. It was a startling experience to stand there and
look up into this huge saucer. Although constructed for track
and football, the Dodgers converted it into a baseball park as
a temporary home while Dodger Stadium was being completed.

I'd never seen anything quite so enormous in all my life.
When full, it seats 100,000 for football and 92,000 for baseball. It's a funny thing about a ball park when you see it for
the first time. The fences always appear closer. With the
now-famous left-field screen only 250 feet away from home
plate, it looked as if you could bunt the ball over it. I found
out later that it wasn't quite that easy.

The screen didn't affect my play too much because with
the predominance of right-handed pitchers in the league I
mostly bat left-handed. On the other hand, it worried a lot of
right-hand batters. Many of them tried to become pull hitters.
If you're used to hitting straight away, it's not easy to change
your style and pull the ball. Wally Moon, who came to the
Dodgers from St. Louis, had his best years in the Coliseum

by putting a golf slice into his left-handed swing and dropping a lot of balls back of the screen for home runs. I would like to have seen Frank Howard powder one clear of the Coliseum. He hit some balls about as hard as I've ever seen, but none of them carried far enough to clear the top row. I suppose it would have been impossible.

Even though the Coliseum was a makeshift ball park it was still home to me. The fans were treated to some exciting games, especially in 1959 when we bounced back from a seventh-place finish the previous year to win the pennant from Milwaukee. The 11-inning play-off game that sent us to Chicago was one of the most thrilling games we played all season.

Most infielders (and outfielders) had a difficult time in the field because of the many physical abnormalities peculiar to the Coliseum. The ground, for example, was hard in some spots, soft in others. The ball took a lot of crazy hops and spins. The Bermuda grass which is fine for football but unsuitable for baseball was like a deep-pile carpet. This slowed the ball down, and many well-hit balls never got out of the infield. This helped me in some respects because I could outrun a lot of grounders. Once the ball hit the dirt, however, I was in trouble again.

The infield was cut too shallow so I couldn't play deep for balls like I could in other National League stadiums. The background was especially poor for day games because of the gray-colored cement and the bobbing white shirts. The outfielders had a miserable time at twilight when they lost the ball in a combination of lights, dusk and people.

It was a big thrill playing before crowds of 90,000. This was a marked contrast from some of the minor-league crowds I'd performed in front of from Class D to AAA. I'd never seen so many people at a ball game before in my life, and I wasn't alone in this respect. The crowds didn't make me nervous. Although I was a rookie, I rather enjoyed their enthusiasm and with everyone rooting the Dodgers on, it made me want to play better. I know most of the fans and the players throughout the league were pleased to see us leave the Coliseum and the historic "Chinese Wall." But we won a pennant there, it was our home park, and it was still major-league baseball that was being played.

A comparison between the Coliseum and the new Dodger Stadium should not be made. There just isn't any way to describe the thrill I received the first time I entered our new ball park. I came in on the third level. It was so beautiful and so fabulous that it nearly took my breath away. All season long I looked forward to coming to the stadium each day because it was so comfortable and I was so proud to be playing there.

The fans in Los Angeles are the greatest in baseball. They deserve a stadium of their own, and I only hope we can bring them another pennant or two to let them know how much we appreciate their support. It was interesting to note that in our first year in Dodger Stadium, we set a new major-league attendance record. The 2,684,170 figure was more than the runner-up Giants and the third-place Pirates drew combined.

Everything at the new park is ultramodern. Because of the cantilever construction, every seat has a completely unobstructed view of the field. The theater-type seats look so comfortable that I'd like to sit in the stands someday and watch a ball game. It really must be enjoyable. The stadium is located near the heart of Los Angeles and is surrounded by three freeways. The present capacity is 56,000, but the Dodger management in time may increase this to 80,000.

The Dodgers have their executive offices on the Club Level, on the same elevation but at the opposite corner from the exclusive Stadium Club. On the very top of the 124-foot-high grandstand is a public restaurant which affords a beautiful skyline view of metropolitan Los Angeles.

Our own spacious clubhouse is the finest I've ever seen. We have our own meeting room, the trainers have their own quarters, and there's even an infirmary with an X-ray machine.

If a player is injured he can get X-rays taken right in the clubhouse without the risk and trouble of being transported to a hospital. Each of the players has a big locker. There's foam-rubber matting on the floors and in the tunnels leading from the clubhouse to the dugouts. The dugouts are the biggest in baseball. We also have our own intercom system, but no piped-in music.

When we moved over to Dodger Stadium I started playing more like a major-leaguer. Being a line-drive hitter, the large playing area gave me a better chance to run. As a team we couldn't rely on the home run like we did in the short-screen Coliseum. This brought back our running game in which we specialize. The infield was fast so I was now able to hit ground balls through the hole and also beat out a lot of high choppers. On the bases I no longer had to wait for the sign as I did in the Coliseum, and this opened up the game for me, so much so that I was able to triple my stolen-base output.

The groundskeepers completely renovated the field before the '62 season, plowing it up 22 inches and packing the soil so that it would absorb sufficient moisture. Before the inaugural game, the field was flooded with a series of abnormal rainstorms which eventually left the surface unusually hard. This was fine for baserunning, but in handling grounders infielders found the ball often took off when they tried to field them. I'm not making alibis, but on a hard infield it is almost impossible to run over in the hole in back of third base, then set, and throw to first. When your spikes start slipping, you might as well hold onto the ball.

My daily routine was changed somewhat when we moved over to Dodger Stadium from the Coliseum. Up until this time I was only a few minutes away from the park, but Chavez Ravine is located on the north side of the city and requires fighting an occasional freeway jam. I leave earlier now and am about the third or fourth player to arrive each day. That was one of the problems I had when I first came to the Dodgers—being on time. I learned that major-league ball clubs put a lot of emphasis on being prompt. Being on time is a matter of habit; there's really no excuse for being late. Maybe once, but never twice. Many people don't realize why we have to be at the ball park 2½ hours before game time.

The first thing we do when we get to Dodger Stadium is to check the bulletin board for any change in the pregame schedule. We might have a presentation or some type of ceremony planned before the ball game, which moves every thing up five or ten minutes. It's a good idea to get to the park early to allow for these special activities. One of the first men to greet us is John Griffin, the clubhouse manager, who always has two dozen balls for us to autograph.

Our roster of 25 players is always split into three groups. The pitchers hit for about ten or 15 minutes then turn the field over to the utility men or humpty-dumpties as they are affectionately called. When they finish, the starting line-up moves into the cage to hit in the regular batting order. We are supposed to bunt two and hit five or six. This session usually winds up with some player hitting 15, others hitting 20 and upwards. I start off with about six the first time. Then Jim Gilliam might hit about eight. Willie Davis will come along and hit ten. Not to be outdone, Tommy Davis will hit 15. Frank Howard will become impatient. When he gets his turn he'll sock 20. By the time we get down to John Roseboro, the No. 8 man in the order, he's apt to camp in there for five minutes. About that time everyone starts yelling at the hitters and we've got a king-size rhubarb going for us. It's fun though, and it gives us something to jaw about besides the umpires and the other team.

During the last few minutes of batting practice we play a game, "one and one." You get two pitches, either hitting the first or taking. On the second pitch if you get an acknowledged base hit you get an extra swing. If you don't get a hit you have to get out and let the next hitter take his cuts. One of the more exciting games we play is known as home run. If you can hit one out of the park you get another swing. I haven't had any extra swings in Dodger Stadium but I've earned a few in the other ball parks.

The Dodgers carry special batting-practice pitchers on their payroll who come to the stadium and work with us each day. These include former major-league and Coast League stars Clarence Maddern and George Vico and a crafty southpaw named Cliff Craig. Craig is currently employed with the Los Angeles Police Department. He's regarded highly by the players who constantly have warned the Dodger management not to let him sign with any other National League club. He played in the minors several years ago. He's really tough to bat against. He has a herky-jerky motion, throws a lot of sinkers, and has terriffic change of pace. I don't think he realizes how deceptive he is. He should talk to Jim Gilliam. Gilliam forfeits his turn at bat when he's on the mound. He hasn't been able to touch him.

Another top batting-practice hurler is Carl Barringer. He's been with us now for the past two years. Barry was one of the leading pitchers in the Dodger farm system, but for some reason never made it to the big leagues. He's in the majors now because he travels with us and is an important member of our organization. I think it is a fine thing for the Dodgers to give him this opportunity to "play" in the National League after so many good years in the minors.

Just before the game starts we take infield practice. Pete Reiser drills the ball around from third to first. While this is going on, two other men stand in the big white circles off the first- and third-base lines lofting fungoes over our heads to the outfield. We take two ground balls which we throw to first; then we throw the ball around the infield and work on the double play. When the weather is hot I'll take an abbreviated drill and let one of the reserves or extra men wind it up for me at short. Most of the other infielders do the same thing because it's important to conserve your energy. If it's humid and you had a late night game the previous evening, or if you've been traveling, these infield workouts can take a lot out of you.

We also have a classy second infield with some of the utility men and the outfielders coming in to play the various positions. Big Frank Howard is my relief at short. I try to get off the field as inconspicuously as possible because at six feet seven inches he makes me look like a Little Leaguer when I stand alongside of him. I'm always getting on Frank about chopping up the infield and causing bad hops for me, but he claims he's as light on his feet as a ballerina. I've never seen a 240-pound ballerina; have you?

We had a lot of fun in the clubhouse after each game we won during the 1962 season. Andy Carey had a camera and took shots each night of the players who were instrumental in winning that particular game. To be in the picture, you had to be one of the stars of the game and you also had to come up with some goofy costume or hat, the crazier the better. You may have seen some of them in the *Life* magazine article on the Dodgers. The pictures were posted on the bulletin board. At the end of the season the player with the most points received a special gift.

We also were awarded extra points for noteworthy performances. For example, I picked up three points when I broke the stolen-base record and four when I reached one hundred. As simple as these pictures appeared, they created a lot of interest and gave each player an added incentive to be "mugged" each night. These same photos were sold at the concession stands in Dodger Stadium enabling the fans to participate in our fun.

One of the largest scoreboards in baseball is located high above the stands in right field. It is operated electronically and keeps the fans up to date with a running account of the game. It has the batting orders of both ball clubs and the customary balls, strikes, outs, runs and hits by teams by innings. Another giant installation known as the "message board" is located above the left-field pavilion. Scores of all the games played in the majors are flashed periodically along with other interesting

chapter 16

South for the Winter

My INTRODUCTION TO winter-league ball came in 1953 when I received an offer while playing shortstop for the Dodgers' Pueblo farm club. Jackie Robinson headed our team and we barnstormed on an exhibition circuit through the South facing the Indianapolis Clowns of the U.S. Negro American League. Jackie had lined up a strong club of major- and minor-leaguers including Gil Hodges, Luke Easter, Ralph Branca, and Bobby Young to name a few.

One of my top thrills came in my very first game on this tour. We were playing right outside of Baltimore, and a lot of my friends and all of my relatives came over to see me play. I didn't start, in fact, I sat on the bench for nine innings.

"Jackie, half the people in the stands came here to see me play and I haven't even made an appearance," I kidded him from the bench.

"Gosh, Maury, I didn't realize you haven't been in—get up there and hit for me," he ordered.

So they announced on the public-address system that I was batting for Jackie Robinson. Here I was only three years out of high school and I was batting for my boyhood hero, the man I considered one of the biggest stars in baseball!

It would make a better story if I could report that I doubled or tripled for him, but that wasn't the case. I flied out to center field.

The next day it dawned on me that we already had a short-stop and that I'd better find another position, otherwise I might wind up selling tickets or handling the equipment. This same day we needed a starting pitcher so I told them I had originally been signed by the Dodgers as a pitcher and that I thought I could get the job done. So they gave me the ball and I went out and won my first start. I also won the next five, and when we left the States I had a record of 6-0. My control was good, I didn't walk too many, and in getting the ball over the plate consistently, each game I pitched took less than two hours to complete.

When we wound up our tour in this country, we headed for Mexico City where we played a three-game series with Bobby Avila's all-star team from Vera Cruz. I pitched one of the games and wound up on the short end, 1-0, even though I threw a one-hitter. Three weeks later I accepted an invitation to play in the Mexican winter league and became a member of the Leon team, a city about 300 miles from Mexico City.

It was tough enough trying to beat our opponents, but one of the biggest enemies we faced was the "Aztec two-step," also known as diarrhea. The change of climate, different food, different water—things were not the same as at home. Most American ball players fell victim to this malady, and it wasn't anything to joke about. I've seen some poor fellows lying in bed for days, so limp and weak they could hardly open their eyes.

When I broke in with the Leon club, I did so as a pitcher. For some reason I couldn't locate the plate. It might have been the altitude; I don't know what caused my sudden wildness. It was hard to accept. Until this time, control had been one of my greatest pitching assets. Just when they were about to release me and send me home, they gave me a trial at first base. I handled the assignment satisfactorily, and hit over .300.

This opened the door to another winter in Mexico in the same league but with another ball club, Cordoba, in the state of Vera Cruz. I played shortstop and led the league in stolen bases, triples, doubles, runs scored, and was second in hitting.

Diarrhea isn't the only thing that can hold you back in Mexico. The language barrier also presents its share of problems. When I first joined the Leon team, the only three words I knew were *juevos con jimon,* so I ate ham and eggs three times a day for two weeks. I also learned *cafe con crema* (coffee with cream) which helped a little. In desperation I bought a small dictionary and learned one new word each day. Then as I improved I learned two words a day. Within a month the other ball players thought I had gone to school in Mexico; they were impressed with my ability to order anything on the menu.

In reporting to Leon, I flew to Mexico City and expected someone from the ball club to meet me. I followed instructions and stayed at the Regis Hotel. After two days, when no one showed up, I started running low on money. I thought I'd better be on my way and report to the ball club so I hired a cab. I figured the fare wouldn't be too high and that the club would pay the bill. Not knowing the distance to Leon, I was amazed when I found out it was over 300 miles. At that, the cab fare was only 300 pesos or $24.00, which should shake up a few of the cabbies in New York and Chicago. My arriving by taxi really rocked the other ball players when I told them I came all the way from Mexico City. I later learned that the conventional means of intercity transportation was by bus.

If you've never been on a bus ride in Mexico you haven't lived. I nearly didn't either. All roads in Mexico lead to and from Mexico City. The best way to travel, like it or not, is by bus. Unfortunately, some of the roads pass high into the mountains and are only wide enough for one bus, not two.

You can imagine the suspense and drama when two buses meet head on on a precarious curve with no guardrail and a 500-foot precipice dropping sharply to a canyon below. At night it's even worse because they only have their parking lights lit. They'll take the curve at 50 or 60 miles an hour without slowing down.

It's become so difficult to rescue the victims in some areas when a car or a bus goes over the side that highway officials have placed headstones in memoriam at the site of the accident. It makes you realize how safe air travel can be. In spite of the difficulty and the hazardous conditions, in my opinion, Mexico has the finest drivers in the world.

In most towns there are few stop signs, only traffic circles and no lights. The cars zoom around the circles practically on top of one another and yet none of them collide. It's unbelievable the way they race through the streets at night with their lights off to save their batteries. If it's completely dark they might turn on their parking lights, but if there's one street light they'll turn them all off. When they stop for a traffic light they turn their engines off to save gas.

The buses always were crowded with people, chickens, owls, baskets, bundles, and luggage of every possible description. It was always a relief to stop for hot coffee. Elevation in Mexico City is about 7,500 feet, so it is cool and crisp there most of the year. We had our own bus when I was with the Cordoba team, and this was convenient until it broke down—about every other day. When it broke down, the heating system would go off, and we'd spend most of our time trying to keep from freezing. We'd put our uniforms on over our clothes, our warm-up jackets, towels, anything we could get our hands on to try to keep warm. We even made a fire inside the bus one day. Stopping for coffee was a poor way to keep warm when the heat wasn't functioning. About then all I could think of was my nice warm home back in Washington.

There's a ruling that after a player has been in the major leagues for two years he cannot play winter-league ball in

Latin America. The Latin players are permitted to play because they live there. With the leagues right in their own backyard the fans would be mighty bitter if their own native players were unable to participate. I personally wouldn't want to play any more. Right now, I couldn't stand the pace. My primary reason for playing as a minor-leaguer was to support my family during the off-season. I couldn't make this kind of money at home, so it was a good solution at the time. My only regret was being away from my family so much of the year. The experience proved invaluable to me, and I know this was a contributing factor when I finally made it to the big leagues. I know now that I'm a major-leaguer; I'll never take anything for granted. When you come up the hard way you appreciate what you have. It's like a wartime experience: you wouldn't want to go through it again, but having done it you're glad you did.

Some clubs send players to the winter league to gain experience. This is what the Dodgers did with Frank Howard. He can't play there any more because he's been in the majors over two years. Many of the first- and second-year men play in Latin America to augment their regular-season salaries. It takes awhile after getting into the majors to get on your feet financially. Whether you make $8,000 a year, or $80,000, everyone expects you to act like a major-leaguer. You have to dress like one, tip like one, and behave like one. The money these younger players make during the winter-league helps them over this financial hump.

A lot of strange things can happen to you when you're in a foreign country. One day I was sitting in the lobby of our Mexican hotel reading a magazine when three policemen came through with rifles and marched me off to jail. I had no idea what was going on, but I wasn't about to argue with three armed guards. I found out later that I was supposed to have made some uncomplimentary remarks about the government of Mexico. This way my first and, I hope, last time in jail. It was more like a dungeon. It was so dark that I couldn't see two inches in front of me. There was one little window at the top of the wall which let in a crack of light. The place smelled like the city dump on one of its worst days. I heard somebody move so I knew I wasn't alone. I didn't move a muscle and didn't dare take a deep breath. I wasn't scared—I was petrified. I sat in the corner and tried to relax, but it was impossible to do so. Finally one of the owners from the ball club came and released me. I definitely was upset. When I returned to my hotel room it was five in the morning. My roommate who had been asleep wanted to know where I had been. When I told him I'd been in jail, he couldn't believe it. He wanted to know why, so I told him I had been accused of making derogatory remarks about the Mexican government. Right then I knew that he was the one they were after, not me. We had had some financial problems with the team, and my roommate sounded off in no uncertain terms as to how he felt about Mexico and the way he had been treated.

One of the early drawbacks in playing winter-league ball in Latin America was in getting paid. Many of the owners claimed the gate receipts were insufficient and they'd hold up the paychecks until enough admissions had been collected. My roommate and I refused to go to the ball park one time because the owners were two days late in paying us. The owners came over to our hotel and practically begged us to appear. They promised us that they would pay us after the game. We agreed to play. We were instrumental in winning the game, but when it was over there was no sign of money. The next day we remained at our hotel. The team lost. After the game the owners tracked us down and paid me but not my roommate. This was when he blasted the government, and I was taken to jail. I can laugh about it now, but at the time it was a rather grim experience.

Salaries and playing conditions have improved considerably since those pioneer days of winter-league ball. The various leagues have joined together with minor leagues in the United States to form a federation. This organization protects the ball

players who play there. Each Latin country must deposit a
specific sum of money in advance with a central office. This
also protects the club owners by preventing ball players from
jumping the club and going home.

The pay in Puerto Rico averages about $1,000 a month.
In Venezuela it goes as high as $1,500 including living ex-
penses. My first year in Mexico I received the equivalent to
$400 a month and expenses. This looked good to me because
it was a little more than I had been making in the minor
leagues in the United States. As I advanced in classification, by
the time I started playing in Puerto Rico I was up to $1,000 a
month. Man, I thought I was stompin' in tall cotton.

In Puerto Rico I played for a town called Mayquez. It's
about 2½ hours by bus from San Juan and may have the
biggest ball park in the world. It's over 400 feet to left field,
some 600 feet to center, and nearly 400 feet to right field.
Even though Mayquez is a religious town, the fans are really
rabid. They're called *fanaticos* and are well named. When
Juan Pizzaro pitched a no-hitter in an opposing town in
Puerto Rico, the fans became so enraged that they broke every
window in his team's bus. Car windows also are broken after
some of these games.

The fans support their home teams in a big way, and I enjoyed a strong following at Mayquez. It all started with my
first game, which eventually led to my signing with a team
in Venezuela. The owner of the Venezuela team had turned
me down even though the manager and the coach had urged
him to sign me. I didn't have a big name at the time, and he
was primarily interested in name players. Following my first
game in Puerto Rico I received a telegram from the Venezuela
owner apologizing for not hiring me. He had read in the
paper where I got three hits, a home run, a triple, and a
double, scoring the tying run, and drove across the winning
run.

I had a big year in Puerto Rico playing shortstop. I led the
club in everything but home runs. and I was second in that

department. We played four or five games a week including
Sunday double-headers. Some of the better-known players in
the league at the time included Orlando Cepeda, Jose Pagan,
Joe Christopher, Vic Power, and Pizzaro. Tommy Davis and
Frank Howard played in the same league in later years.

After Bobby Bragan had encouraged me to switch hit in '58,
I went to Venezuela at the end of the season to polish my left-
handed hitting. I played for one of three teams in the city of
Maracaibo. The name of the team was Pastora. The owners
were among the finest I ever had met. They always paid us
on time, often taking us to the bank to help us make out drafts
so we could send money home. One man in particular, Lucas
Rincon, is one of the best men I've ever played for in professional baseball.

One of the clubs we faced was Cabimas, managed by Pete
Reiser and made up of a lot of Dodger farmhands as well as
some of my own teammates from Spokane, among them Larry
and Norm Sherry, Charley Smith, and Tommy Davis. The
way Larry Sherry pitched to me, you'd think that we were
strangers. He was there to help me find out if I could get out
of the way of a pitch. He warned me not to dig in against him.
After getting a hit and stealing a base my first time up, he
advised me to stay loose. Knowing Larry, I took his advice.
He came close, in fact, too damn close. After brushing me
back twice I knew that getting out of the way would not be one
of my problems. I wouldn't say he was trying to hurt me, but
he was definitely aiming at my body.

Just to let Larry know I wasn't going to roll over and play
dead, I singled off of him for the second time. I stole second
again, and he informed me that he was going to let me have it.
Right after that I stole third, and he was really fuming. As we
changed sides I went to Pete Reiser and said, "You'd better
have a talk with Larry. He's trying to hit me."

"Oh, no, he's only kidding, Maury. He wouldn't do a thing
like that."

I've always trusted Pete, but his word then wasn't accurate.

When I came to bat, Sherry decked me two straight times. But to show him I was still a sport, I singled for the third time and stole my fourth base of the day.

We still joke about this incident. It was in fun. I know Larry wasn't throwing at my head because that's how serious and permanent injuries occur. He was just brushing me back to stop me from planting my rear leg. That's part of the game. This is the way I like to play. I respect Larry for feeling the same way.

I found that the fans in Venezuela were just as rabid as the ones in Mexico and Puerto Rico. They're also great gamblers. They'll bet on every pitch. If you win a ball game the fans pick you up on their shoulders and carry you through the streets of the town to your hotel. It's best not to try to get away because even though they're a friendly mob, they might become insulted.

It's also advisable to lose as few games as possible. When we did drop one, police would come on the field and stand shoulder to shoulder facing the crowd while we tried to slip through to our taxi without getting pelted by sticks, rocks, fists, and bottles. Sometimes they tried to tip our cab over. The driver often drove away with several people hanging all over the car.

One year in Venezuela I stole 40 bases in 41 attempts. The protest the fans put up when I was thrown out on my 41st attempt defies description.

"*Que pasa?* . . . *Que pasa?*" (What happened?) they screamed at me. For a moment I thought they were going to tear me apart but fortunately I lived to play another day.

chapter 17

Inside Baseball— Tips and Secrets

MAJOR-LEAGUE INFIELDERS can't always go by the book. It looks simple enough to the average observer, but there's a lot to think about and do on each play. For example, I have to play one way behind one pitcher and a different way behind another one. With Sandy Koufax throwing his blazing fast ball I shade all hitters to the opposite field. I'll get two steps closer for a right-handed hitter.

With Johnny Podres on the mound I play the hitters to pull more. If he's facing a right-handed batter I'll fade a couple of steps toward third because Johnny throws a lot of breaking balls and an assortment of slow stuff.

With Don Drysdale pitching I play the batters straightaway. Don has a good fast ball, but he doesn't have the blinding speed that Koufax possesses. He doesn't throw as much junk as Podres. He mixes his pitches pretty well, and I play in a regular position.

When Ed Roebuck comes in for relief duty I play the right-handed hitters to pull more toward third. Roebuck throws a lot of sinkers and tries to force the batters to hit the ball on the ground. When they do hit the ball they're apt to pull it.

You not only have to adjust your defensive play with each pitcher, you also must make allowances for the condition of the infield surface itself. At Dodger Stadium I play deeper than in most parks. For one thing the ground is hard and the ball gets to you in a hurry. During the '62 season it was difficult to go over into the hole in back of third and slide into the ball with your right foot because the ground was so firm it wouldn't give. With the field renovated I'm now able to make this play as it should be made.

Candlestick Park's soft infield slows down grounders, and I have to play shallow. If you're too deep, fast men like Mays and Pagan will beat out ground balls.

It's just as important to know the other team's hitters as it is to know your own pitchers. This is something you have to learn. When I first joined the Dodgers I thought it would be impossible to remember the habits of more than 200 different ball players. It's not difficult at all. After one time around the circuit you know about everything there is to know about a rival player—his likes and dislikes—whether he prefers Western movies to whodunits, whether he takes his coffee black, and, of course, his batting strength and weaknesses. We have clubhouse meetings and review each individual batter.

These meetings are an important part of baseball. The coaches and Alston sit up in front of the room with the players seated in front of them. Pete Reiser gets the line-up of the opposing team, and we'll take each player individually and the pitches that he hits best. Then we'll discuss the ones he's weak on, whether he can bunt, how fast he can run, how well he throws, if he charges the ball in the outfield. If he's an infielder we'll discuss how well he makes the double play, or any little thing that might help us.

After we've reviewed the regular line-up and the utility men we'll take a look at the pitcher. We find out if he's a fast-ball pitcher or a curve-ball pitcher. We keep charts on each team. The pitcher scheduled for duty the following night has this assignment. If the hitter makes an out, it's recorded whether he was retired on a low, inside pitch, if it was a curve ball, where he hit it, and how well. If the batter got a base hit, we'll chart that; also which type of pitch he hit, which field he hit it to, and how hard the ball was hit.

We also keep lifetime batting records of all the players in the National League. For example, if Willie McCovey is hitting over .500 aaginst Don Drysdale we mention this and try to find out why (so does Don). We'll go over the chart and find out the pitches he's had the most success with. If he's been hitting fast balls, then we start giving him change-ups and curves. If he's been effective against the slow stuff we pitch him fast balls. He might be hitting fast balls inside so we'll pitch him fast balls away.

Each Dodger's lifetime hitting record also is tabulated. For instance, a player like Duke Snider may be on the bench for a week but in reviewing his file we might find that he's had a lifetime average of .485 against a certain pitcher. More often than not, we'll make a switch in the line-up to let Snider bat against this pitcher and play in this particular game. We've been keeping these statistics ever since I've been in the majors. It was a relatively new idea at the time, but it's standard practice now.

It's helpful to know the abilities of your opponents. You want to know how fast a man can run—if he gets away from the plate quickly or if he starts slowly—you have to know the instant the ball is hit just how hard it's coming to you and how much time you have to charge it, field it, and make an accurate throw to first. With players like Bill Virdon of the Pirates, Felipe Alou of the Giants, Vada Pinson of the Redlegs, and other fast men you've got to get rid of that ball in a hurry.

An important phase of infield play is to know the outfielders playing behind you. I have to know just how fast Willie Davis can come in on a fly ball so there won't be a collision. As an infielder I must know how far back I can run. I also have to know how far out I must run to take the relay. This depends on the throwing strength of each outfielder.

One of the most exciting plays in baseball is the double play. When executed properly its precision is beautiful. It can really take your pitcher out of a tight situation. There's no set way for the shortstop or the second baseman to make the double play. Probably the most conventional method for me is the crossover. I catch the ball while I come toward second and then following my throw I wind up on the right-field side of the bag. If a player is sliding toward my legs, I leap out of his way and throw after first tagging the base. Another popular way is to take the throw and make the relay from inside the base, or if necessary, I can tag the bag then move backward and make the throw.

It's a good idea to know your base runners; otherwise you may wind up in the middle of left field. There are certain runners who take pride in coming down to second like a fullback trying to score from the one-yard line. Then there are others who come in with a half-hearted attempt to break up the play. We keep a mental book on those who come in easy and those who try to take your leg off. Frank Robinson, Don Hoak, Ken Boyer, and Eddie Mathews are among the players who like to slide hard and attempt to upset you. Mathews hit Neal so hard in the Coliseum one night back in 1960 that Neal was out cold for ten minutes. Another time Robinson caught Don Zimmer with his spikes and ripped his pants from his knee to his belt.

When we face hard runners we remind each other to step in and cheat a step so you get the ball quicker and get it to the pivot man sooner. Once you receive the ball before the base runner gets to you, you have the latter at your mercy—he's got to slide. Sometimes they can't get low enough. You aren't going to throw at them deliberately or try to injure them, but at the same time it's a good idea to let them know they'd better stay low.

The throw to first off the double play can be made overhand or underhand. When I joined the Dodgers I employed a three-quarter-overhand throw. I soon learned that I would have to come underhand to get the base runners to slide, otherwise I wouldn't last long on the double play. This was something that Neal and Zimmer taught me. Most base runners know the infielders who will throw underhand or overhand on the double play.

It's imperative that you know how to make all the pivots. If the runners find out you can only go one way they'll know how to slide to take you out of the play. It's a good idea to mix them up; in this way they can't follow a pattern and they won't be able to break up the double play as often. When the runner is right on top of you, you've got to pivot out of the way.

There's plenty of pressure on the base runner too. I remember back at the Coliseum in 1960 I hit Orlando Cepeda of the Giants right between the eyes. He was late getting down in starting his slide. The ball hit him just above the bridge of his nose and bounced about 50 feet in the air. It scared the hell out of me; I thought I had killed the poor guy. He had to leave the game and missed the game the following night. He was restricted to his room at the Ambassador Hotel. I stopped by to see him the next day to let him know it was accidental in case he had some doubts. It goes without saying the next time he came into second base he hit the dirt in a hurry. After you start throwing underhand on the double play you never give it a second thought. You expect the base runner to get out of the way.

In making the double play, one of my biggest problems, when I first became a major-leaguer, was to give Charley Neal a ball he could handle. The first thing you must do in fielding a double-play ball is to let the pivot man see the ball at all times. He's got enough to think about with the base runner bearing down on him to start hunting for the ball. If he has trouble locating the throw from the shortstop then he's not going to make the double play consistently.

You'll see us feeding the ball to the pivot man out of our gloves. This is not the recommended way to make the play. It's better to give him a firm underhand toss so he can see the ball all the way. After keystone men work together for several years they know exactly what each one is doing. Then they can get away with some of the unorthodox mannerisms, but it takes months of practice to know where the ball is coming and where the pivot man will be.

When you have to go deeper in the hole, an overhand throw is often required. This throw also can be made side-arm or underhanded, but it's got to be a firm throw. It can't be lobbed nor thrown so hard it will be difficult to handle.

After playing a season with Charley Neal I knew every move he made around second base. Even though he made different pivots he still liked the ball in the same place every time, right at his chest. He preferred the ball a little to the inside of the bag. Gilliam likes the ball lower and directly over the base. This affects your fielding, which is one reason a manager tries to get a set combination as early as he possibly can. You have to be sharp because when you make plays in the infield most of them are done instinctively—you don't have time to think whether it's Neal or Gilliam or Joe Blow. It's something that must come naturally.

In throwing to first you have to give the first baseman a ball with a lot of zip on it. I like to keep my throws low around the knees or waist. In this way the first baseman can stretch out for the ball and shorten the throw several inches. Baseball, like other sports, is often a game of inches, and while it might seem unimportant at the time a bad or mediocre throw can cost you dearly. If you throw high to first and the first-sacker has to leave the ground or even stretch high to catch it, a fast runner might beat the play. It helps to have a first baseman who can lean out for throws.

I try to grip the ball across the seams. In making the throw to any base, especially the long throw to first, you have to be careful that the ball doesn't sail or sink. It all depends on the way the ball spins. When you throw sliders, curves, or breaking balls, you always throw the ball off center. If you do this on your throws to first, the first baseman is going to have a problem. That's why I grip the ball across the seams so the ball will rise. A good throw to first base is one that will rise and carry. During a game we don't have time to look in our gloves to see if we are gripping the ball across the seams. With practice we do this automatically. I go right to my glove, grab the ball, and by the time it leaves my hand I have my fingers across the seams. This is a good skill for younger players to perfect during warm-up throws and practice sessions.

There are several ways to tag the base runner. Some infielders like to straddle the bag; I prefer to take the throw on the inside of the base. If I'm straddling the bag and the base runner is a guy like Frank Robinson he'll come down and jump right on my chest. John Roseboro throws on the first base side of the bag, and if I'm straddling it I'm going to be in trouble. With the runner bearing down on me I'm going to have to lean into him to catch the ball on the inside of the base. I have to cut across in front of the base line to catch the ball and tag the runner. I try to make a sweeping tag and jump out of the way all in one motion. The one thing I try to avoid is contact. You can get your shins pretty well chewed up when you tangle with some of these 210-pound bruisers; they can cripple you with one blow. Also it's hard to hold onto the ball if you're rolling around in the dirt. So I try to make a clean tag with the back of my glove and get out of the way.

The rundown is a play which requires hours of practice. As simple as it seems, it's one of the tougher plays to make in the infield. The best way to play the rundown is to make as few throws as possible. This can even mean getting the runner without any throws at all. If a player is clever enough he can fake the throw and make the tag unassisted. I laugh every time I think of Dick Stuart at Pittsburgh a couple of years ago. He had me picked off of first, a cinch out. Anxious to make the play without throwing the ball, he chased me all the way to second, and I had a stolen base.

Infielders should keep the ball in sight at all times. It should be held high and to the side. Any throw besides the first one is one too many.

In practicing relays from the outfield, we learn that if the ball is a sure double not to cover second base, but to back each other up to prevent the base runner from continuing to third. If there's a man on first you want to keep him from going home. We worked this play so well that when we saw a throw coming in that was going to be difficult for the relay man to handle he'd step aside and let one of the players backing him up catch the ball on a perfect hop.

This requires teamwork and practice—you've got to know the men you're playing with and how they position themselves on hits to all fields. A heads-up infielder will do everything he can to prevent the base runners from advancing. Rather than just standing there watching the game, if it's a play where I'm not involved I might run over to back up the first baseman or I might go all the way home to cover a play. This is what it takes to win ball games.

One of the key plays we work on is the pick-off. When executed properly it can take a pitcher out of a tight spot and prevent the other club from having a big inning. One of the problems in starting a pick-off is getting the pitcher to look at his infielders. With men on base, the pitcher is more concerned with the batter and often concentrates so much on the pitching that he forgets to see if there is a chance for a pick-off. I'm constantly reminding our pitchers to look. Even with the opposing pitcher at bat I like to work the pick-off play because some pitchers can hit. Then if the play works you might have this same pitcher coming up as the lead-off man the next inning, and this is an ideal situation.

The pick-off signal can be given by the catcher or any of the four infielders. We use any number of signs such as taking the glove off, touching the cap or face, tugging at the belt, or picking up dirt. You also have to know your runners to pick a man off base. Bad runners are seldom caught; they're too cautious and don't take a long enough lead. The average fan might think that Willie Mays or I can't be picked off because we're good base runners. Actually we're the type that can be nipped because we take the extra lead.

Baseball has a sign language all its own. On the Dodgers we probably run through at least six sets of signs a season. Signs can be picked up by the other team so you must be careful in giving and receiving them. Because some players are slower picking them up a coach has to repeat himself, and the other team is apt to break your code.

Most signs are basic, so a player with good baseball savvy shouldn't have too much difficulty deciphering them. The important thing about signs is that there's a key. A coach might go through a million gyrations but until he gives the indicator, they don't mean a thing. After the players master the signs they don't have to think about them and they can concentrate more on hitting or base running, whatever the case may be. Some managers will give a hit sign; others will not.

There are countless ways to flash signs. The Cardinals, for instance, could establish an entire code based on the color red. They wear red sweatshirts, have red belts, red beaks on their caps, red birds and red letters on their shirts. Their coach might use the tip of his nose as the indicator and the first thing he touched which was red after that would mean to bunt.

I've known players who have trouble remembering signs. They can remember fundamentals which are much more complicated, but they have a hard time fixing signs in their minds. We review signs constantly in the clubhouse. The manager emphasizes their importance. He constantly reminds the players to learn them as well as they possibly can. Signs can mean the difference between victory and defeat, and it's amazing how many are missed each season—not only on the Dodgers but on every other major-league club as well.

Some players and coaches are exceptionally talented in picking up signs so you can't be too careful. A base runner at second can look right at the catcher at the same time the pitcher is getting his instructions. With situations like this, the catcher uses a series of signs. If a sharp base runner can pick up a sign he can relay it to the batter, and the latter has a much better chance of getting a hit if he knows what type of pitch to expect.

On the pick-off play, if the pitcher acknowledges your sign, then you know he's going to throw the ball to you. If he ignores you, it either means he didn't see your sign or, if he did, he doesn't want to attempt the play at this particular time. Roger Craig is one of the better pitchers to work with in attempting a pick-off. Several times I'd give him the sign while he was in his stretch and he'd answer me—almost like a quarterback coming up to the line of scrimmage and changing his signals to take advantage of a defensive maneuver.

We also have signs with the catcher on throws to second. On one sign he'll call for a pitchout and throw to second; on another it's optional whether he throws to second or returns the ball to the pitcher.

It's important for us to be alert on the bases and to steal as many signs as we can. There was a particular game in 1962 when we were being shut out, 3-0, and had hardly touched the pitcher. There were two outs when I connected for a double. I picked up a sign, and before we knew it we had six runs that inning. It proves how important this phase of the game can be. You've probably read about the binocular incidents, the spyglasses from center-field scoreboards, and others. It's difficult to minimize the value of knowing what the other team is going to do even though this is a sneaky way of getting information.

Of all the assignments on a ball club, I think coaching at third base is the toughest of all. When you have a running ball club like the Dodgers with men like Tommy Davis, Willie Davis, and myself running at top speed, Leo Durocher has his work cut out for him in giving us our instructions. He's got to use peripheral vision, keeping one eye on the ball and the other on the base runner. If it looks like the ball will be back in the infield he's got to hold us up. When you have a man who can run as fast as Willie Davis you can't be indecisive because Willie has so much momentum you have to start slowing him down in time or he'll overrun the bag. Leo has to make a snap decision. If he should wave him home it's too late to bring him back to third. This is a highly responsible job.

Leo and I teamed up in the second play-off game in Dodger Stadium when Ron Fairly hit a fly ball to short center field. Leo knows that Mays has a powerful arm. It was a difficult decision to make.

"Tag up! Tag up!" he barked at me.

I can watch the ball, too, and if I wanted to go home and Leo told me not to go then I could become confused. I might not get as good a jump. As soon as he gave me the green light —and I knew that I should be running—it gave me a strong incentive to beat the throw. It's important for the coach and the base runner to think the same way. They have to work together. If you're on first and there's a ground ball through into right field your eyes belong to the third-base coach only. He's the one who lets you know whether to stop at second or continue to third. If the play is close at third you'll notice him getting a line on the throw and motioning the base runner to slide to the opposite side of the base, away from the ball.

Leo has to be careful not to let a base runner get trapped in a rundown. This can cost a team an important run, especially in the middle of a rally. When a coach sends a runner home and the catcher has him out by four or five feet this can be a little embarrassing when 55,000 people are watching. Then the coach looks like a bum. If the ball should be wide or get past the catcher then the coach is a hero.

He also has to give signs so the opponents can't follow them. He's got to be clever enough to throw the sign stealers off guard. Sometimes in an obvious situation like a two and two count, he'll flash the take sign knowing full well that the batter isn't going to be taking.

Every time things get rough playing shortstop, I think about Leo Durocher coaching at third. I wouldn't trade jobs with him if they paid me double!

chapter 18

Wind, Mud, and Willie Mays

THERE'S SOMETHING IN the air besides Dodgers when we fly to San Francisco to play the colorful Giants. It's difficult to describe, but there's a definite tension in the air. It reminds me of a homecoming college football game. There's just something that happens—a feeling of electricity each time we face San Francisco that is different than any other National League series. It's the old rivalry of the Brooklyn Dodgers and the New York Giants taking place all over again on the Pacific Coast. Although there are few of the old pros left from the eastern rosters, the bitter competition still exists.

As we leave the airport in south San Francisco we can spot Candlestick Park from our bus windows (if it's a clear day) because the park is at least a mile from the Bayshore Highway. If the fog is too thick you can't see the divided white line let alone the baseball stadium. Candlestick Park provokes a lot of wisecracks from the Dodger players. The park itself isn't exactly a baseball paradise, what with the winds blowing in six different directions and enough water in the infield to float a small battleship.

If we have a night game we go directly to the Palace Hotel

on Market Street in the heart of the financial district. If it's a day game we'll go directly to the ball park. When you enter Candlestick Park you are impressed. It is a beautiful, symmetrical arena situated on the side of a scooped-out hill and located on Candlestick Point which juts out casually into San Francisco Bay. The grandstand is of cantilever construction which (like our own Dodger Stadium) means that there are no pillars or posts to obstruct the spectators' view of the field. On a clear day (they do have a few) it is a beautiful setting.

The visiting clubhouse is very plush with carpeting on the floor, roomy and fully equipped with every modern convenience. The runway from the clubhouse leads right out into the Dodger bullpen. Everything is great, big league in every respect.

Then comes the shock treatment. When you try to get on the field, it's like walking into a blizzard. I have to put my shoulder to the door and shove with all my might to get out. This actually happens at Candlestick Park. If I'm not careful the door can slam back on my arm or leg and I could be seriously injured. Once I get it open I sort of jump out real quick and then it bangs and makes an awful racket when it closes.

The wind is so strong it jams the door shut in a hurry. Then when I come out on the field I'm right down at the Dodger bullpen on the Giant side of the field. This is something the Giants inaugurated a couple of years ago, which is a good idea. In this way each bench faces its respective bull pen, and the coach can signal for the pitchers he wants to warm up without making a big production about it.

An important part of our pregame warmup in Candlestick Park is for Pete Reiser to hit us high fly balls to see if we can catch them in the wind. If I'm at shortstop when the ball starts upward I usually catch it back in medium left field or shallow or medium center field. You never know where the ball is going to land. Rather than make the play like it should be handled on any ball popped up behind the infield or right

behind second base, the shortstop will go out while the second
baseman covers the base, or vice versa. But in Candlestick
Park we all have to go out and surround the ball because we
never know where it's going to fall. We let the pitcher cover
second while the rest of us play a game of roulette as the wind
blows the ball in five different directions. We never know
who's going to catch the ball. It keeps us on our toes. Another thing, it makes us appreciate our own ball park even
more. With all the confusion and commotion over the Coliseum, nothing could ever be as frustrating as Candlestick
Park. It's in a class by itself!

As I leave the Dodger bullpen I have to lean into the wind
to work my way down into the Dodger dugout. The Giants
will be taking batting practice so we have to cross in back of
their batting cage where all of the San Francisco players are
huddled waiting their turn to bat. We usually stop and ex-
change a few remarks with them. I chat with Orlando Cepeda
awhile and Willie McCovey mumbles a word or two as if it
were an effort to open his mouth. Jose Pagan, Felipe and
Matty Alou gather around and then when Willie Mays trots
over, the show begins.

Just about this time the reporters start gathering to pick up
something they can latch onto for a story. We often walk
away. If that doesn't work, we just split up. I remember
during one of the '62 playoff games a photographer wanted to
take a picture of some of us talking, but we wouldn't permit it.
Fraternizing with the other team is against the rules. But as
long as you aren't out on the field hugging each other, no one
is going to object too strenuously. You are permitted to ex-
change a few thoughts with your opponents and then move
along. There's a pleasant atmosphere existing between the two
clubs even though we're bitter rivals. We were exceptionally
friendly before the play-off series started but once the first
pitch had been thrown we were at each other's throats. But
while good sportsmanship and a buddy-buddy relationship had

existed all season long, when the play-offs began there was bad feeling between the two teams.

Individuals were squaring off, and there was little love lost anywhere on the field. Orlando Cepeda and I had always been good friends on and off the diamond.

"You really turned out to be a good hitter," he told me one time I reached first.

"You're pounding that ball hard these days. You're looking good up at the plate," I'd remind him when he reached second base.

But all this chit-chat came to an abrupt end when we tried to subdue the Giants in the crucial three-game set that was to decide the National League championship. Cepeda had nothing to say to me. I returned the favor by giving him the silent treatment. I have a feeling he may have been peeved at me for picking him off second. The play took the Giants out of a big inning, and I know it made him angry.

I remember another incident which occurred when I hit a ball down the first-base line that the pitcher fielded and threw to Cepeda for the out. Rather than tag the base he hit me fairly hard in the chest with his elbow. Normally he'd barely touch me when he made a tag, but this time he hit me hard and hit me high. Another time when I got on first he yelled at Jose Pagan in Spanish to hit me between the eyes if I didn't come in low enough on the double play.

Even Willie Mays, the good-will ambassador who always said, "Say, hey!" was not his usual affable self when the play-offs began. There were thousands of dollars riding on every pitch, and I think the Giants as well as the Dodgers were starting to count their World Series money. So the thought of winning the play-offs and meeting the Yankees in the World Series was taking on added importance. The horse play which had prevailed all season long was forgotten as we settled down to the serious and dramatic side of settling the campaign.

For some reason I always seem to be at my best when we're playing the Giants. This is an ideal situation because the

Giants are the team to beat. Back in 1959 when the San
Francisco club was still playing in Seals Stadium, the old PCL
park, we took on the Giants in what later proved to be the
turning point in the season. When we came to town we were
two games behind them; when we left we were one game in
front, and the Giants had had it. This was to be my biggest
series of the '59 season. Up until then I was barely batting my
weight. I had even thought about asking the Dodgers to send
me back to the minors. When we arrived for this crucial
series, I noticed a sign in the Giant clubhouse that said, ONCE
YOU QUIT, YOU'RE FINISHED!

I don't want to get maudlin, but this made such an impression on me that I decided to give it my best for at least another
month. Apparently this was a good omen because the following day one of the reporters told me I was starting. As mentioned elsewhere this one series probably did more to boost my
stock as a Dodger than any other performance that season. I
wasn't particularly fired up for these games. It just happened
that everything I touched turned to gold. I happened to be involved in nearly every key play, either scoring an important
run or batting it across. Another time I would get the lead-off
hit that led to a must run. I led a charmed life during these
three games. I could do no wrong. Success didn't come to me
one day too soon, because along with everyone else I too was
giving up on Maury Wills. An example of how things break
for you occurred when I was at bat and missed the take sign.
Instead, I swung away and hit a line-drive single to center.

Aside from winning the trip to Japan, which was a tremendous thrill, I got another big charge when the photographers took a picture of Wally Moon, Gil Hodges, and me
swinging our bats. I always had been considered a good glove
man but a weak hitter. And here I was along with two of the
top sluggers in the game receiving recognition as a hitter. It
was almost too much! This is a picture I'll save to show my
grandchildren.

After this big series, many of my Dodger teammates started

to call me Tiger, quite a compliment. They had called me Mousey when I first joined the club. My reputation as a Giant killer started with this 1959 series, and it seems that every time we've played the Giants since then I'm supposed to turn in a superhuman performance. In a way this thought gives me added incentive to excel, and if playing conditions improve a little, I may do even better.

It's far from easy to give a superior effort in Candlestick Park. Most ball players are at their best in warm weather. You avoid sore arms, and your muscles and joints are lubricated by body fluids which this heat generates. It's cold and windy in Candlestick Park most of the time. My fingers get so numb I wear golf gloves. Then I wear two pair of sanitary sox besides my regular blue stockings. I also wear long, insulated underwear, an extra-long-sleeved woolen sweatshirt, and a thin cotton undershirt. On top of this I wear a turtleneck sweater and my uniform, so you can see I have added weight which isn't conducive to stealing bases.

If all this weight wasn't enough of a handicap, the wind blowing from left to right field is enough to give you an inferiority complex. Of course, if I do happen to get on first I have to wade through the mud to get a jump toward second and believe me that takes some doing.

I raised such a ruckus over the muddy infield when we played there in August, 1962, that I was thrown out of the game. This was only the second time I had been ejected in the major leagues. I had previously been tossed out in Philadelphia on a close play at first base. I flung my protective helmet high in the air in disgust. The umpire said, "If it hits the ground you're out of the game." You should have seen me trying to catch it. However, I failed and was tossed out of the game.

The infield watering episode at Candlestick Park proved to be one of 1962's biggest baseball controversies. It received nationwide attention and even though I was thrown out of one of the games I still feel that I have a beef coming. The Giants know that we play a running game and they knew that a heavy

infield would slow us down on the bases. I don't really blame
the Giants for doing this; in fact, I think it was shrewd of
them. I don't think they expected to get away with it, but
they did, so more power to them. I personally feel that someone in authority should be blamed for letting them turn the
field into a quagmire. But I'm just a player and not a very big
one, so perhaps it wasn't up to me to voice my opinion. But
I did speak up for what I thought was right. As a result, I was
asked to leave the premises.

If the Giants wanted to shake us up they couldn't have
picked a better way to do it. We were really demoralized. It
even affected our hitting because we were so angry over the
mud we couldn't concentrate properly at the plate.

Everything started out innocently enough. When we took
the field for batting and infield practice the ground was perfect. The wind was blowing like it always does, and, aside
from the infield grass which was four inches high in some
areas, the rest of the diamond was well groomed. With fifteen
minutes remaining until game time, we went into the clubhouse to relax, change our undershirts, and have a soft drink
or a cup of coffee. We were sitting around making small talk
when one of the players came running in screaming:

"You should see what those damn fools are doing to the
infield!" We rushed out on the field. The San Francisco
ground crew (I call them the Giants' demolition team) had
brought out their big hoses and had watered the field so
thoroughly that there were actually puddles on the skin part of
the infield, and the game was scheduled to start in two minutes!
The baselines from home to first and from third to home were
perfect but the ground between first and second and second
and third was so muddy that you couldn't walk without sinking
to your ankles. This was the first time it had happened, and
Jocko Conlan ordered them to fix the field. They went through
the motions and dried it out a little, but it was still mushy.

The next time we played there the same thing happened.
Unfortunately, there was another group of umpires and not

one of them had the fortitude to assert himself to get the Giants to improve the conditions of the field. They claimed they didn't have the authority to do anything about it. I felt they should have treated the mud just like they would rain. When it rains, the ground crews come out with rakes and wheelbarrows of dirt and dry out the wet spots. But this was not done.

The last time we were there for the opening game of the play-offs for the National League championship, true to form, the field was sloppy again. Conlan was again in charge, and, after a heated argument with San Francisco manager Alvin Dark, he held up the game for the ground crew to work on the infield. Rather than improve conditions, they actually made it worse. Instead of dirt, they poured sand. When the water soaked through it was impossible to get any appreciable traction. We lost this game, our fourth loss in a row. If this was the way to win ball games, the Giants had the right solution. We were almost whipped before we stepped out in the mud— I mean on the field.

As it turned out, the Dodger players and management weren't the only ones who were upset over the dampened playing conditions at Candlestick Park. Sid Ziff in his column in the Los Angeles *Times* had this observation which disclosed that many fans were also deeply concerned:

CANDLESTICK FLOOD THING OF PAST

It does pay to squawk when you've been given a bum deal. Something has come out of the protests raised by L.A. fans over the outrageous flooding of the base paths at Candlestick Park at the last Dodger series. IT WILL NOT HAPPEN AGAIN on the written promise of Warren C. Giles, president of the National League. Strangely, no announcement ever was made public by his office, but the promise is explicit in a letter to Mrs. Stuart A. Fraser, who wrote a letter of complaint to the league president. This is the reply she received:

"Dear Mrs. Fraser:

I read with interest your letter of Aug. 14 and agree
that excessive watering of the field at Candlestick Park
during the recent Giant-Dodger series was a violation
of the spirit of the rules. I have so advised the San
Francisco club and I assure you that while there is no
rule governing this specific situation now, provisions
will be made to prevent any recurrence of such an act
at any of our parks in the future. I want you to know
that I appreciate your interest in writing.
                              Sincerely yours,
                              Warren C. Giles, president."

Good! It was a bush league, underhanded stunt. Had Giles
allowed it to pass it would have opened the way for all sorts
of shenanigans. The image of sportsmanship would have
been tarnished in major-league ball. It was a helluva poor
show to put on in front of an audience of thousands of kids.

As you may have guessed by now, I haven't exactly been a
ball of fire on the basepaths in Candlestick Park. While I stole
12 bases in 12 attempts against the Giants in '62, most of them
were accomplished in Dodger Stadium. The San Francisco
pitching staff isn't the toughest in the league to steal off, nor is
it the easiest. Juan Marichal is one Giant pitcher who is difficult to run against. Even though he kicks his leg high in the
air, he fiddles around a lot on the mound, throwing frequently
to first. Often I stay tight by first hoping he'll throw home.
He still keeps trying to pick me off. If it got to the point where
we really have to have a stolen base then I think I could steal
off of him. Many times, though, I prefer to let him throw
home and see what develops with the other hitters.

In the final play-off game I was more determined than ever
to steal against Marichal. I put out every ounce of energy
within me. I knew if we didn't win that game there would be
no tomorrow. I probably wouldn't take chances during the
regular season like I took in that final game. I was determined

to go all out, and I stole three bases that afternoon. One of the other players told me that two of the bases were practically stolen before the catcher started his throw. Many times during the year, I would keep a pitcher relaxed by staying close to first, especially if he threw over to the base a lot. Then later in the game when we really needed the theft I would cut loose and make the steal.

Billy Pierce is the toughest Giant pitcher to steal against. I'm working on him, though, and he'll find me more difficult to contain in the future. Oddly enough, Billy Odell, a left-hander, doesn't cause me too much trouble. Even though he's looking right at me I know I can steal off him.

While we resented being on the short end of the stick in our games with the Giants, they are shaping up as a fine ball club. One of the most improved infielders in the league is the man they have playing shortstop, Jose Pagan. He has really come into his own as a major-leaguer. He covers a lot of ground and has an excellent arm. I knew him when we played winter ball in Puerto Rico in 1957. He was in Class AA ball at the time. He's improved immeasurably since then. He is not only a fine player, but a good kid as well. We talk back and forth and I try to encourage him, especially if things aren't going too well for him. I also pat him on the back when he deserves it. Even though we're rivals, if I don't help him, someone else will. I think the day is gone when athletes try to take a man's livelihood away from each other. Everyone wants to win. That's the object of the game, but to try to injure someone deliberately or force him out of his profession—these things don't go in my book.

Another friend of mine on the Giants is Willie McCovey. I knew Stretch when he was with Phoenix in the Coast League. He shuffles along like he has all year, and he's one of the nicer guys in the game. Don't ever ask Don Drysdale to say anything nice about McCovey, however. His lifetime batting average against Big D, the leading pitcher in baseball in 1962, is right

around .500. So if Don never sees Willie again, it will be too
soon.

One of my favorite people is the great Willie Mays. They
just don't come any better as a person and as a player. Just to
be around him and talk with him one never would think he's a
superstar. He certainly doesn't try to remind you that he's
Willie Mays. He's just a regular guy. To be named Most
Valuable Player over him is as big an honor as winning the
title itself. To think that I was selected over a ball player of
Mays' caliber is more than I ever dreamed would happen.

This reprint from the December 15, 1962 *Sporting News*
will show you what I mean about Mays being a big person:

"MAURY DESERVES IT," DECLARES MAYS, RUNNER-UP IN MVP RACE

Willie Tips Hat to Dodger Swifty—Predicts Drop in His '63 Theft Total

By Jack McDonald

San Francisco, Calif.

Ever since he came into the league in 1951, Willie Mays
has had a virtual "copyright" on the MVP award, at least
he's the man to beat, and many of his admirers think this
recognition should have gone to him in the Giants' pennant-
winning year, 1962.

But not Willie. "I was glad to see Maury Wills get it,"
said Mays, who finished second, commenting on the award
for the first time. "He deserved it for having beaten Ty
Cobb's long-standing stolen base modern record."

The Dodger theftician stole 104 bases. Mays stole 18, but
led Wills by a wide margin in home runs, 49 to six, and runs
batted in, 131 to 48.

But Mays forsees a falloff in Wills' thefts in 1963. "The
pitchers will throw more to first base and the catchers will be
more alert when he's on," said Willie. "They will never stop

him from stealing a lot, but they'll figure out ways to slow him down."

This is really something. Only three or four years ago I was hoping and praying I could play well enough to become a major-leaguer, and here I am—selected over a big star like Willie Mays as the Most Valuable Player in the National League. I can't believe it yet!

Whenever we invade San Francisco the games are apt to be sold out a week or two in advance. Unfortunately, it's tough to get passes for these games. We'd like to get a few extras now and then for some of our Bay Area friends. These same people invite me to dinner, but I seldom accept. Most of the time we stay close to our hotel room and rest. If we lose, we aren't in a mood for conversation; if we win, we're usually too emotionally or physically exhausted. It's always a big series, and, while we aren't unsociable when we play the Giants, it's worse than a hard day at the office. There aren't too many laughs. We're all business because it's a case of all work and no play. Once in awhile I drop over to the Red Garter to check the banjo music, and now and then we enjoy dining in one of the fine San Francisco restaurants.

Most of the sportswriters and a good many fans gave up on us when we were shut out in the opening play-off game with the Giants, 8-0. Frankly, if we're going to lose, we'd rather get whipped by a wide margin than say 1-0 or 2-1. Those are the games that tear you apart inside because you normally have two or three chances to go out in front. Or you might have made a key error or a mental mistake that cost the game. We were thoroughly thrashed, but we were determined to forget about it and concentrate on the game coming up in our own stadium.

What troubled us the most was that we were in one of our worst slumps of the season. We had gone runless three straight games; in fact, up until the time we scored in the second game we had gone scoreless 35 consecutive innings. When we broke the drought we did it convincingly, scoring seven runs in the big sixth inning.

It didn't come an inning too soon to suit any of us. We were really depressed. But as soon as we scored all these runs the Dodger bench came to life and we looked like the Dodgers that had set such a torrid pennant pace all summer. Everyone was talking it up, and with our big guns, Tommy Davis and Frank Howard, getting key hits we were all very much alive. The climax came when I tagged up at third and scored on Ron Fairly's short fly ball to center field. That broke a 7-7 tie and squared the series at one game apiece.

I was mobbed something fierce when I crossed home plate. It was the first time in my career that I had ever experienced anything like this. It actually frightened me because several men were hurting me without realizing it. I remember one fan in particular. I thought he was a photographer because he had something strapped across his shoulders. It looked like a camera, but it turned out to be a pair of binoculars. He had one arm gripped around my neck and was pounding me in the ribs with his free fist yelling, "Thataboy, Maury! Thataboy!" I'd hate to be captured by an angry mob if this was supposed to be a friendly one!

Had I scored the winning run the next day, rather than head for the dugout, I was going to sprint out to center field where they'd have to catch me. Nevertheless, it was a great thrill. When I got to the clubhouse there were reporters and photographers from all over the country who had come to cover the play-offs and the opening games of the World Series. There must have been about 200 men in the room; it was a madhouse. Everyone wanted to know how I felt about scoring the winning run.

It was difficult to explain. I knew that when Ron Fairly hit the ball it wasn't too deep, and that Mays would make the catch in shallow center field. I also knew that our run production was so skimpy that I couldn't take a chance on the next batter bringing me home. It was a contest between Mays and me. Either he would make a perfect throw to the plate, and they'd nail me, or I'd beat the ball to the catcher. I knew I had to get a good jump; I couldn't start late. I'm sure Mays knew it would take a perfect throw to beat me. As it developed the throw was off to the left of the plate, and I knew I had it beat by a safe margin. On a play like this I have always felt that the percentage is with the base runner. As it turned out, the play wasn't even close. In his anxiety to tag me, Giant catcher John Orsino lunged at me without the ball.

This happened on my 30th birthday, and I couldn't have asked for a better present than this important run which beat the Giants.

With the stage now set for the season's finale, it is doubtful if a Hollywood script writer could have depicted a more favorable setting. Here we were at the end of 164 games, all tied up. Each club had identical won and loss records of 102-62. Third-place Cincinnati was 98-64, which in many seasons would have been good enough to take the pennant.

The Dodgers had an added incentive when it was learned that the Giants had put in an order for champagne after they had won the opener in San Francisco. We resented this cocky attitude and were determined to break up their victory party. It didn't turn out that way, but no one will say we didn't try.

That final game still seems like a nightmare. None of us could understand how it could happen. When I scored the fourth run in the bottom of the eighth and we went out in front, 4-2, all we could see were dollar bills floating around in front of our dugout. I was already counting my World Series money, and I know most of the other Dodgers were counting theirs. I was planning my trip to New York where I had been signed to make several television appearances. It's too bad the game didn't end an inning earlier. When the ninth inning was over and we staggered into the clubhouse on the short end of a 6-4 count, the gloom was so thick you could cut it. Some players were crying; others were in a stupor. A few players stayed in the clubhouse and didn't leave the stadium until 11 o'clock that night.

Just thinking about that final game depresses me. All we needed were two outs, but we couldn't hold the lead. It would have climaxed a tremendous season. I got four hits that day to extend my total to 208 and also stole three bases, winding up with 104. These were incidental to winning the pennant, then and now.

Although we went down to defeat, I have to admire the Giants. They were apparently hopelessly beaten and yet managed to come up with four runs when every one else had written them off. It was the second time the Giants had given the Dodgers the business in a play-off. Back in 1951, Bobby Thomson hit his historic home run in the ninth inning to win the flag for Leo Durocher's club. I have nothing but respect for the Giants and their courage and ability to come back when everything was stacked against them. A club like that showed a lot of class and deserves the recognition they received as champions. Regardless of how poorly we played, you can't take anything away from them. The pressure was on, and they still came out on top.

The Los Angeles sportswriters were put out with us because we kept them out of the clubhouse for nearly an hour following the final play-off game. After losing a game which we had won, the last thing we wanted to do was talk about it. They were pretty bitter and felt they should have been admitted sooner. We wanted to be alone in our darkest hour. We were criticized for going into seclusion, and perhaps rightfully so. I don't know how it feels to die, but that's about as close as I want to come for a long while.

While the second guessers are having their innings, I can look back on the '62 season with a great deal of satisfaction— not only personally but from a team standpoint as well. I think we played and acted like pros all season long. There was Don Drysdale, the No. 1 pitcher in baseball with 25 wins; Tommy Davis leading the league in runs batted in with 153 and in hits with 230; Frank Howard taking over as a regular in June and still hitting 31 home runs; Sandy Koufax injuring his finger early in July and yet striking out 207 batters; Ed Roebuck and Ron Perranoski having a great year as relief pitchers; and I had the best season I ever had in my life. Yes, I think we have a lot to be thankful for and should still be able to hold our heads high.

I'm sorry we let the fans down because they were with us all the way, right up through the last inning of the last game. Usually when you win 102 ball games you also win the pennant, but not in 1962. But that's baseball, and that's why it's such a great game. We have a solid young ball club, and many of its stars will be heard from for many years to come. I'm sure we'll all benefit from this experience, and with a lot of fine prospects coming along from the minors, we'll be tougher than ever throughout the '60s.

chapter 19

Guest Star—
Charlie Dressen

DURING THE WINTER of 1962-63, I renewed my friendship with one of my former coaches, Charlie Dressen. Charlie has returned to the Dodgers, and we're glad to have him back. When he learned that I was writing this book he asked if he could add a chapter. Not only am I grateful for the kind things he has said but it's one less chapter I had to come up with myself.

Take it away Charlie Dressen—

In the case of Maury Wills, I think it was a fortunate thing for him to eventually wind up with the Dodgers. I remember when the Detroit club was interested in his contract. At the time, the Dodgers appeared solid with men like Bobby Lillis, Don Zimmer, and Charley Neal all available for shortstop duty. Wills would make the fourth candidate for the position. So rather than hold a man back, the Dodgers agreed to let the Tigers take Maury on a look-see basis.

The man who negotiated the deal was John McHale who left Detroit to become president and one of the principal stockholders in the Milwaukee Braves. Had McHale remained with the Tigers, Wills would probably be in the American League today. This was a good break and the kind that often happens in baseball. When Wills came to the Dodgers the Coliseum was against him as far as stealing bases was concerned because of the short left field fence. Now that the club is in Dodger Stadium, stolen bases are of utmost importance.

I've heard this kicked around since he stole those 104 bases, and many baseball observers have analyzed this feat in many different ways. I think the value that most men have overlooked is that when a man steals as many bases as he did, he had to get a lot of singles, and when you're on first base with no one out or with only one out, there's a chance that the batter will hit into a double play. So anytime you steal second you eliminate that double-play danger. I don't think this has been brought out. It's tremendously important because the double play can kill a baseball team. In some games a team will hit into as many as three double plays, the equivalent of two complete innings. It has to hurt.

One thing I liked about Maury when he joined the Dodgers back in '59 was that he listened to advice and constantly tried to improve himself. I showed him how to make the relay play and several other tips that he has profited by since then.

I told Maury after he had his record-breaking season that he was going to be asked a million questions. Reporters and fans are going to run him ragged, and many of them will ask him the same questions over and over again.

I know he's a pretty level-headed kid and that he won't make the mistake that some players in the past have made in playing big shot with the press. I told Maury to answer any and all questions like a man. Some will be silly, but every newspaperman in both leagues is interested in Maury's opinions and is entitled to know what he thinks about these various baseball subjects.

Wills is a quick runner. I've watched him. He'll take about three steps and he's going at full speed. His own teammate,

Willie Davis, can outrun him; I saw it happen at Dodgertown, but there's more to stealing bases than speed alone.

That's what I liked about Jackie Robinson as a base runner when I managed him. He wasn't real fast, but if you blinked your eye or looked the other way he'd be on second base.

I've been asked how Wills compared with Robinson. It's difficult to rate the two because they are two different types of players. Robinson was much larger and not as fast as Wills, but he was a daring type of player who always made the opposition work to get him out. Jackie hit a lot of long balls. Wills has relied more on line-drive singles and ground balls through the infield.

Being the first Negro to play in the major leagues, Robinson went through a lot of experiences that players don't have to face today. He ducked his share of beanballs, but I never heard him holler. He also antagonized the other ball club and often forced it into mistakes. I know there are plenty of National League pitchers who would like to see Maury in the other league. I think I'd get pretty upset if I was a pitcher and Wills stole base after base against me.

I was looking forward to seeing Wills and the rest of the Dodgers in the World Series. I know they would have done as well against the Yankees as the Giants did because pitching is so important in a short series.

It's really something to play 162 games and at the end of the season find two teams as evenly matched as the Dodgers and the Giants. I think that's pretty good baseball. I know many baseball men I've talked with feel that Maury's many stolen bases helped keep the Dodgers alive when they needed a shot in the arm. His feat of stealing 104 bases added a lot to the game. I sent him a telegram following his 104th theft, telling him the thrill I experienced in watching him take the headlines away from brute strength. Most any one can hit a home run. Every one's swinging for the fences. And there are some big, strong bruisers in the game who are a lot more powerful than Maury Wills, but not one of them can steal that many bases. The Toronto papers carried a day-by-day account of his activities in headlines. It wasn't uncommon to pick up a paper and read *Wills Steals Two More.*

As I watched on television while the Dodgers' pennant chances faded in the last inning of the last game with the Giants, it was history repeating itself. When I managed the 1951 Dodgers we had the Giants on the run, and it looked like we were home free. We had knocked their ace, Sal Maglie, out of the box and were sailing along with one out in the ninth when Bobby Thomson ripped into a pitch from Ralph Branca.

If you've ever been to the Polo Grounds, you know what a great distance it is from home plate to the clubhouse in deep center field. Well, the walk I had to take that day was the longest one I ever took in my life. It's long enough when everything is going well. But I knew I had to walk those "five miles" and that I had to talk to the players, which I did when I got out there. I told them that they were a fine club, that it was a tough thing to get beat on just one pitch, there was nothing to be ashamed of, and they went down like champions. They had proved themselves the previous Sunday in Philadelphia when they won after being behind five or six runs. Jackie Robinson made a diving catch to save the game, then won it in the 14th inning with a home run. The Giants had already won their game, so we had to beat the Phillies to force a playoff.

Mr. O'Malley came into the clubhouse after I finished talking to the team to praise them. He told them not to worry, that they had done a good job. He also told them that I was going to be their manager the next season.

Now that I'm back with the Dodgers for the fifth time I think this time I'm here to stay.

I hope I can help the club and that we'll be so far out in front of the other teams these next few seasons that there won't be any more playoffs until the 1970s.

chapter • 20

A Helping Hand

ONE OF MY main objectives in writing this book is to try to help younger players. When a person acquires a certain knowledge, I think it is selfish for him to keep it to himself. It took me eight years in the minor leagues to climb the baseball ladder, and now that I'm in the big leagues I'm still learning.

If there are a few things that I've learned along the way that can be shared I'm happy to pass them on to others. There aren't too many shortcuts to success. Given a certain amount of natural ability the rest is up to the individual as to how badly he wants success and how far he wants to travel to achieve it.

Baseball can't be taught from a book. It takes team instruction and individual instruction. If I in some small way through this book can help some of these players avoid some of the pitfalls that held me back, then I will feel rewarded.

At the same time, I think that younger men should realize what wise men already know—that the climb to the top in any walk of life is not an easy one. Even though the going gets rough we can't put our tails between our legs and run away.

Most any obstacle can be hurdled if we believe in ourselves
and apply ourselves.

I know in my long climb to the majors religion played a big
part. There are a lot of players on our own Dodger club and
throughout the National League that are bigger in stature
and that have more ability than I have. I don't think there's
one of them, however, that has any more inside them than I
do. I don't run any faster now; in fact, I'm slower than I used
to be. I don't throw as hard as I used to. I'm not as quick
as I used to be, and yet I'm a much better ball player. It's
not in my physical make-up—it's in my heart. It's through
my introduction to Christianity through Rev. Charles and my
home church, Mt. Sinai of Los Angeles.

There were plenty of times when I said my prayers right on
the field. There have been other times when I've completed
a key play or made a clutch hit or stolen a base when all odds
were against me. I couldn't have begun to accomplish this
without this spiritual help.

I had this good feeling when I was about to break the record
even though I was facing Larry Jackson, then ace of the
Cardinals' mound staff. Jackson is at his best against the
Dodgers, and every time we played the Cards he was available
for duty. He's been especially rough on me; I don't think I've
stolen more than two bases off him since I've been in the
majors. I don't imagine I've had more than four or five hits
either.

So I was a little apprehensive when I found out that he
would be pitching against us in our 156th game. This was my
last chance to break Ty Cobb's record. I not only had to get on
base twice—he never walked me—I had to steal two bases
after I made it to first.

But with all these odds against me I had a good, warm
feeling that I was going to do it. The second time up I got a
hit and stole second off of him. This meant I had one more
base to steal to break the record. My next time at bat I failed
to get on, so I was down to the wire.

This next time at bat was my last possible chance. I had to get on first and I had to steal second. So things looked a little grim when Jackson had two strikes on me and only one ball. But with everything against me I still had that good feeling that I was going to get on base. I knew Jackson would throw me his favorite pitch, the one which was hardest for me to hit, the slider. This is a breaking ball which comes in on the fists. Sure enough, this was what he threw me and in some way I got the bat around and drove a single between first and second.

Now that I was on first my worries were just beginning. If there's one pitcher in the league who is tough to steal against it's Larry Jackson. He's an expert at holding runners close to the base. I also knew that the last thing he wanted in the world was to have me break the record with him on the mound. The Cardinal catcher, Gene Oliver, also was dedicated to stopping me. He was calling for pitchouts to prevent me from stealing second.

Jackson threw over to first at least five times. He's got a quick move, and I dove back in headfirst. I still felt warm inside and had this same positive feeling that I would steal second and break the record.

It was then that I decided to try a delayed steal. If I didn't break with the pitch, the catcher and the infielders would relax and I would have a better chance to arrive safely. If I left for second with the pitch every one would be watching me and my chances would be considerably reduced. The dugout would be yelling, the shortstop and the second baseman would be ready for me, and the entire Cardinal team would roll into action to chop me down.

When Jackson delivered toward the plate and I didn't break, all attention was focused on Jim Gilliam, the batter. When I did start for second, I was halfway there before they realized that I was running. The shortstop had dropped his hands but was now charging toward the base at full speed. He couldn't catch the ball on the dead run, and I went in head-

first with my 97th theft. It broke the record which had existed
since 1915.

All I could think of was this feeling within me. It wasn't
because I had a good night's rest, because I hadn't. Nor was
it because I had a good rubdown before the game, or because
I had a good sandwich or a special supper. I know that it
was God, and that this was His way of communicating
with me. He was telling me to believe in myself. I thanked
Him then as I had all season long for letting me break this
record. This is something I couldn't have done by myself. I
easily could have broken a leg or sprained an ankle or become
ill, but only because of His goodness and graciousness was I
physically sound all season long. Kids have asked me time
and again how they can steal bases or how they can become a
good shortstop or a good hitter. What I really feel like telling
them is to believe in God first. With a spiritual background
and just mediocre ability a person can go a long way. In my
opinion, I don't come close to having the ability of Willie
Mays or many other players in the league, and yet with help
from above I had a season that earned me the Most Valuable
Player award in the National League.

As for the future I don't see how the Dodgers can miss. I
know we'll be the team to beat. Of course, this depends on
the kind of breaks we get. When Sandy Koufax was sidelined
in 1962 it hurt us, but this is something that happens in
baseball. We've got a lot of great young players, men like
Tommy Davis, Frank Howard, Willie Davis, Ron Fairly, Don
Drysdale, Koufax and a good crop of youngsters who will be
coming along from the minors.

When I think of these young players advancing to the
Dodgers it makes me want to try even harder because I know
if I let down or relax there's someone waiting to take my job.
This is not the time to "Cadillac." That's why I practice constantly. I've had reporters laugh at me for coming out and
practicing on a hot morning on the road when we had a
game that same night. I was hitting over .300 at the time and

starting every game. It's just a belief that I have. I don't
see how a player can improve his game by relaxing. I want to
hold on to what I have, and to my way of thinking the best
way to do this is to not let up for a second.

Several fans have asked me how it feels to be a celebrity.
The word itself just bugs me. Through my entire career I've
never lost consciousness of where I came from and the struggle
I had to get through the minor leagues. This has stayed with
me. I never take anything for granted. I know that everything
that God has given me—and He's given me a great deal—can
be taken away from me as quickly and easily as it was given.
I still feel that people like you and respect you for what you
are, not what you do. I can be the greatest ball player who
ever lived, but that's no sign that I'll be the most popular. I
don't think of myself as a celebrity. I act the way I do, which
is the only way I know how. I've always been this way. It's
the way I am. I just want to be a regular Joe, to live a normal
life like everyone else.

I'm not a crusader, but I feel that we all as individuals have
certain obligations. I'm obligated to God, to my family, my
country, my parents, my race, my ball club, and to myself.
I'm also obligated to mankind. Some people may feel they
want to improve things in the world as far as equality is concerned by picketing, by sitting in restaurants, by riding buses.
I don't feel this is what I want to do. I feel that I can fulfill
my obligation and make things better by being the finest ball
player I can possibly be. In this way I can win the respect of
people, and by carrying myself in a proper manner I can
improve conditions for my entire race.

As for base stealing, I don't imagine I'll ever have another
year to equal the one I had in '62. Like they say in show
business, "It's a tough act to follow." I've asked myself several times, "What can I possibly do for an encore?"

chapter • 21

My No. 1 Booster

GERTIE WILLS, MY wife, has always been one of my most loyal supporters. It hasn't been easy on her—raising five children with me away from home the better part of each year—but I've never known her to complain. Now that we have won some honors and awards I know she also feels rewarded. As far as I'm concerned none of these would mean a thing to me if I wasn't able to share them with her.

I asked her to contribute this last chapter, because I feel she has more than earned a right to speak her piece. If people think I have worked hard to reach the top, it's nothing compared to the 24-hour-a-day effort which she has put in for so many years.

The life of a baseball player's wife is very rewarding; not only from a salary standpoint but from the experiences as well. From Class "D" ball all the way up through the minors to the major-leagues, these memories will never be forgotten. To me the game of professional baseball has in many ways seemed like a ladder. Once you are fortunate enough and good enough to be selected by a major-league scout, the first step of the ladder is placed before you and the farther up you go, the steeper they get.

Maury and I married quite young and by the time he had signed his first contract with Hornell (Class "D") we had one child and were expecting our second. As most of the other players were young, we had more kids than any of them. This was usually the case on every team where Maury played, and Maury was often the youngest player, too.

It was during Maury's early days at Hornell that our daughter, Mauricia, was born. The townspeople took up a collection in the stands and sent it to me. It was sincerely appreciated, because Maury wasn't making too much, even though he sent most of his salary home. We had to stretch our money to take care of the doctor bills and the babies that came to us so very frequently.

After the birth of our second son, Bump, who arrived while Maury was in his second year at Hornell, I went there to be with Maury for the remainder of the season. The inconvenience of the bus trip there was minimized by the knowledge that I hadn't seen Maury since he left home in March for spring training. I think I would have gladly walked there.

This was the first time I had ever seen Maury play professional ball. When Maury hit a home run that day, the tears started streaming down my face. All the other wives looked at me in disbelief but being understanding women they all started crying with me.

Just when I was looking forward to having Maury home for the winter (1953), he heard from Jackie Robinson who invited him to play with his all-star team on a tour through the south. It was then that I first realized the emptiness of being without Maury during the winter and the Christmas holidays. Even if I felt like crying, I didn't have the time, as our three babies kept me on the move. Without the children it would have been much more difficult. Maury was very thoughtful to write and phone long distance, because he knew how much I depended upon hearing from him. He wrote each day and while the phone calls were a luxury, it kept us closer together as a family. When he returned the first winter, he had enough money to last until his first payday along with presents for all of us.

Ever since Maury's first professional game I have kept a scrapbook. I subscribed to the local newspaper in each town where he played and each day I put in a clipping along with postcards which he mailed to us plus any pictures which we took. I started this when we were in high school where Maury was so active in sports. Along with the gold footballs, which meant we were going steady, he also turned over his scrapbooks to keep articles from the local paper. We still have these books even though the paper is getting brittle.

Even though we were a long way from the majors, during our early days in the minors we both had this great ambition for Maury to eventually get to the top but we never talked about it. We watched a lot of players drop out of baseball. They may have lacked the faith, or the drive, which wasn't unusual because the pay was low, and with families to support there were many other ways to make a better living.

Following a good year at Hornell in 1953, Maury was assigned to Pueblo, Colorado (Class A) for the '54 season. After buying winter clothing for all of the children and shipping them ahead of us, Maury phoned three hours before we were to leave for Pueblo to tell me to cancel our reservations. He had been told to report to the Class "C" Miami Sun Sox. Even though the ball club in Pueblo forwarded our clothes they were too heavy for the warm climate and we were still waiting for our first payday. The housing wasn't too sharp but it was wonderful being with Maury, which helped overcome any other minor obstacles.

There was a segregation problem in Miami, as there was in other southern cities. I wanted to go shopping downtown one day but Maury came up with a good idea to keep me from going. He told me in all sincerity that the last Negro who went downtown didn't come back. I think it was an idea he had to save money. Anyway, I refused to go even though he insisted because he felt we needed specific items. Still, I wouldn't budge further than the neighborhood stores and we survived the summer. Once I told a friend, some three months later, what Maury had said and it became the joke of the neighborhood. As I was only 19-years-old at the time and never having been that far south I had every reason to believe him. We still get a laugh out of it today.

The children adjusted to Maury's being away from home so much better than I did. They seemed to accept the fact that he was supposed to be away a lot, playing ball. They liked to look through magazines and when they saw a ball player they would always call him "dad."

From Miami we finally got to Pueblo and I enjoyed living there with the children and attending many of the games. One of the worst things that happened was the time he was hit in the eye when the ball took a bad hop. I was listening to the game on radio and it went off just as he was hit. I was unable to learn anything more about him until he returned home late that night. When I opened the door he had a huge black eye which frightened me terribly. Another time, after a night game, I opened the door and he was wearing a rubber mask. I had hysterics!

As Maury moved up in classification I noticed the "Gold Glove" award which *The Sporting News* presents each year to the outstanding major-league fielders. I mentioned this to Maury each year and he told me he would bring one home when it meant the most. Finally in 1961, Maury received one for his fielding achievement. I know how important the Most Valuable Player award is to Maury as well as his many other honors such as "Athlete of the Year" (1962) but this first trophy has a special place in our home, as well as in our hearts, because I know how hard he worked to earn it.

After Pueblo, Maury went to Ft. Worth, then back to Pueblo, then to Seattle of the Coast League. I tried to join him on occasion, which meant juggling the kids around between relatives until we finally settled in Seattle. We then had four children. It was evident that Maury was making progress up the ladder. He knew it meant working harder to get to the top which called for extra hitting and fielding practice. He realized he had to be a better hitter or he'd never make the majors.

In 1958 when Maury was sent to Spokane, I flew there from Washington D.C. with our five children and at the first sight of this area Maury and I knew this was where we wanted to live and raise our family. It is a most friendly town. The kids loved it from the start and it was a relief to me to know we wouldn't have to be moving each year.

Even though Maury was turned down following a tryout with Detroit at the start of the 1959 season, neither of us was discouraged. Maury worked harder than ever and didn't lose faith for a minute. One day in early July he phoned me from Phoenix to tell me that the Dodgers had sent for him and that he was finally going to the big leagues. I was so happy I was speechless. This was what we had waited for all those years in the minors. Instead of relaxing I became worried and nervous.

Although he got off to a slow start he came around fast toward the end of the year helping the club win the pennant and the World Series from the Chicago White Sox. To see Maury in the World Series was like a dream come true because this was what he had hoped for, for a long time.

Once Maury became a Dodger he worked even harder to remain the club's No. 1 shortstop. Every time there's a Dodger game on television, the kids and I stay glued to the set. He's had some of his best days while we've been watching. Up until the start of the '63 season only Mikki, our oldest daughter, has seen her dad play major league baseball from the stands.

None of the honors Maury earned after the 1962 season can compare with Ty Cobb's stolen base record which he broke. Our youngest son Bump, has decided that the record will